Thomas Novak

Functional Safety and System Security in Building Automation

Thomas Novak

Functional Safety and System Security in Building Automation

A Common Approach

Südwestdeutscher Verlag für Hochschulschriften

Impressum/Imprint (nur für Deutschland/ only for Germany)
Bibliografische Information der Deutschen Nationalbibliothek: Die Deutsche Nationalbibliothek verzeichnet diese Publikation in der Deutschen Nationalbibliografie; detaillierte bibliografische Daten sind im Internet über http://dnb.d-nb.de abrufbar.
 Alle in diesem Buch genannten Marken und Produktnamen unterliegen warenzeichen-, markenoder patentrechtlichem Schutz bzw. sind Warenzeichen oder eingetragene Warenzeichen der jeweiligen Inhaber. Die Wiedergabe von Marken, Produktnamen, Gebrauchsnamen, Handelsnamen, Warenbezeichnungen u.s.w. in diesem Werk berechtigt auch ohne besondere Kennzeichnung nicht zu der Annahme, dass solche Namen im Sinne der Warenzeichen- und Markenschutzgesetzgebung als frei zu betrachten wären und daher von jedermann benutzt werden dürften.

Verlag: Südwestdeutscher Verlag für Hochschulschriften Aktiengesellschaft & Co. KG
Dudweiler Landstr. 99, 66123 Saarbrücken, Deutschland
Telefon +49 681 37 20 271-1, Telefax +49 681 37 20 271-0
Email: info@svh-verlag.de
Zugl.: Wien, TU, Diss., 2008

Herstellung in Deutschland:
Schaltungsdienst Lange o.H.G., Berlin
Books on Demand GmbH, Norderstedt
Reha GmbH, Saarbrücken
Amazon Distribution GmbH, Leipzig
ISBN: 978-3-8381-0956-5

Imprint (only for USA, GB)
Bibliographic information published by the Deutsche Nationalbibliothek: The Deutsche Nationalbibliothek lists this publication in the Deutsche Nationalbibliografie; detailed bibliographic data are available in the Internet at http://dnb.d-nb.de.
 Any brand names and product names mentioned in this book are subject to trademark, brand or patent protection and are trademarks or registered trademarks of their respective holders. The use of brand names, product names, common names, trade names, product descriptions etc. even without a particular marking in this works is in no way to be construed to mean that such names may be regarded as unrestricted in respect of trademark and brand protection legislation and could thus be used by anyone.

Publisher: Südwestdeutscher Verlag für Hochschulschriften Aktiengesellschaft & Co. KG
Dudweiler Landstr. 99, 66123 Saarbrücken, Germany
Phone +49 681 37 20 271-1, Fax +49 681 37 20 271-0
Email: info@svh-verlag.de

Printed in the U.S.A.
Printed in the U.K. by (see last page)
ISBN: 978-3-8381-0956-5

Copyright © 2010 by the author and Südwestdeutscher Verlag für Hochschulschriften Aktiengesellschaft & Co. KG and licensors
All rights reserved. Saarbrücken 2010

Table of contents

1. Introduction 3
1.1 Building Automation and Control Systems 3
1.2 Functional Safety 5
1.3 System Security 9

2. Motivation and Possible Solution 15
2.1 Motivation and Problem Statement 15
2.2 Possible Solution of Common Approach 20
2.3 Scope of the Thesis 24

3. Safety and Security in Today's Automation Systems 27
3.1 BACnet 27
3.2 KNX/EIB 29
3.3 LonWorks 31
3.4 Safety Related Automation Systems 33

4. International Standards 37
4.1 Safety and IEC 61508 37
4.2 Security and the Common Criteria 41

5. Survey on Safety and Security Approaches 45
5.1 Harmonizing Safety and Security 45
5.2 Lifecycle Approaches 47
5.2.1 Terminology 48
5.2.2 Generic Model 50
5.2.3 Safety 51
5.2.4 Security 52
5.3 Conclusion 54

6. Common Approach 57
6.1 Pre-design 58
6.2 Design and Installation 71

 6.3 Operation, Maintenance, Decommissioning 79

7. Key Ideas of Common Approach **87**
 7.1 Safety-security Lifecycle 87
  7.1.1 Motivation 88
  7.1.2 Macro- and Micro-Processes 90
  7.1.3 Safety First 92
  7.1.4 Safety-security Functions 93
  7.1.5 Validation and Verification 94
 7.2 Relationship between Safety and Security 96
  7.2.1 Conflict Resolution Approach 97
  7.2.2 Measure Assessment 102

8. Safety-security Requirements **109**
 8.1 Scope of Use Case 109
 8.2 Definition of the Concept 111
 8.3 Safety Dependent Activities 113
 8.4 Security Dependent Activities 117
 8.5 Safety and Security Integration 123

9. Software Realization **131**
 9.1 Hardware Architecture 131
 9.2 Design 133
 9.3 Development and Testing 139
 9.4 Installation and Operation 145

10. System Integration **151**
 10.1 Gateway and Network Management Device 151
 10.2 Node Configuration and Commissioning 155
 10.3 Node Operation and Maintenance 158

11. Conclusion and Outlook **161**
 11.1 Results and Benefits 162
 11.2 Further Procedure 165

References on Scientific Publications **169**

Internet References **178**

Abbreviations

1oo2	One out of two
1oo2D	One out of two with diagnostic
2oo2	Two out of two
2oo3	Two out of three
ACU	Advanced coupler unit (KNX/EIB)
ADV	Assurance class, development
AES	Advanced encryption standard
ANSI	American national standards institute
API	Application programming interface
ASHRAE	American society of heating, refrigerating and air conditioning engineers
B-AAC	BACnet advanced application controller
BACS	Building automation and control system
BCU	Bus coupling unit (KNX/EIB)
B-OWS	BACnet operator workstation
B-SA	BACnet smart actuator
B-SS	BACnet smart sensor
CAN	Control area network
CC	Common Criteria (IEC 15408)
CEN	European committee for standardization
CIA	Confidentiality, integrity, availability
CRC	Cyclic redundancy check
DC	Direct current (fault model)
DC	Diagnostic coverage
DES	Data encryption standard
EAL	Evaluation assurance level
EHS	European home system
EIA	Electronic industry alliance
EIB	European installation bus
EIBA	EIB association
EUC	Equipment under control
FAU	Functional security class, security audit
FDP	Functional security class, user data protection

FIT	Failure in time
FPT	Functional security class, protection of the TOE security function
FSP	Functional specification (assurance family)
HBES	Home and building electronic system
HVAC	Heating, ventilation, air-conditioning
IEC	International electrotechnical commission
IEEE	Institute of electrical and electronics engineers
IP	Internet protocol
ISO	International standardization organization
ISR	Interrupt service routine
LAN	Local area network
MAC	Message authentication code
OSP	Organizational security policy
PP	Protection profile
RCV	Trusted recovery (functional security family)
RMF	Risk management framework
SAR	Security audit review (functional security family)
SCADA	Supervisory control and data acquisition
SDI	Stored data integrity (functional security family)
SFF	Safe failure fraction
SHA-1	Secure hash algorithm 1
SIL	Safety integrity level
SNVT	Standard network variable type (LonWorks)
SOF	Strength of (security) function
ST	Security target
STM	Time stamps (functional security family)
TC	Technical committee
TLS	Transport layer security protocol
TOE	Target of Evaluation
TUV	Technischer Überwachungsverein
V&V	Validation and verification
WG	Working group

1. Introduction

Automation systems are technical systems that perform a given task in order to relieve human beings. They can be distinguished by their purpose or by their application. The first means differentiating between direct – taking over a task – and indirect support – optimizing the environment. In the beginning of integrating automation systems the intention was to (partly) substitute human work by automation systems because they do a job more accurate, faster, more reliable, less expensive, with a higher level of quality and so forth. Think of employees at the train station who were opening and closing the gates when a train passed a crossing. Today's automation systems have replaced them step by step. Another example is an automatic door locking system. It locks the door of a building at a defined time. A doorman who locks each door manually with a key is not required anymore. Indirect support means that the automation system optimizes a secondary process such as a climate control in an office building. They support human beings and try to make their life easier or more convenient.

1.1 Building Automation and Control Systems

Differentiating automation systems by their application, results in categorizing them into automotive systems, industrial automation, building automation and control systems and so on. Automotive systems are systems with a rather limited amount of nodes compared to a BACS. They require the transmission of a message with very short delays in case of a critical situation. They are decentralized systems where a node starts to send when it has to. Moreover, a high amount of reliability of the system must be guaranteed. Finally, transmission errors must be detected with a very high probability and retransmission strategies have to be implemented. CAN (Control Area Network) developed by the company Bosch [ZEL98] in the mid 1980s is the system in the automotive area. It is noteworthy to say that CAN is used in other fields of applications nowadays such as medical engineering or industrial automation [LAW00, pp. 312].

Industrial automation systems are similar to automotive systems with regard to the level of reliability or the number of nodes. They also require robust transmission because of possible electromagnetic interferences and have a static network topology. Like automotive systems they are mostly closed systems not remotely accessible. On the contrary industrial automation systems in general are not very demanding regarding transmission delays. In addition, most of them are centralized systems where each node is triggered periodically to send messages. Examples of industrial automation systems are PROFIBUS [IEC68, type 3], P-NET [IEC68, type 4] or INTERBUS [IEC68, type 8].

Building automation and control systems (BACS), also called building automation systems (BAS) [KAS05], are integrated in today's buildings to improve the interaction among integrated devices and people living and working in a building. In accordance with [DIE97, pp. 17; DIE00, pp. 8; KAS05] building automation is concerned with the control of building services and provide control of conditions of indoor environments automatically. Typical services are heating, ventilation and air-conditioning, subsumed by the acronym HVAC. Others are lighting and shading.

A BACS is, compared to an industrial automation system, different in many ways. Being based on the same principles and technologies the structure of and usage in buildings and the respective services lead to highly specialized systems. Their main features are [BAU00]

- low bandwidth required from end nodes,
- event driven and therefore less regular traffic,
- soft real-time requirements, but
- large number of network nodes (currently up to 50000) [DIE00, p. 10].

While the first three properties ease the life of an engineer, the last one results in a number of problems. Such a high amount of nodes has a massive effect on

- scalability,
- node costs,

- safety and security, and
- engineering tools (network management, commissioning, etc.). Unlike industrial networks, it is not possible to maintain the network manually. Sophisticated tools are necessary to give the operator an overview of the system and to help him making the right decisions when something goes wrong.

The most important aspect is the costs of the individual network entities. The possible high number of nodes and therefore network infrastructure entities can lead to too expensive systems, when they are compared to their benefit. The benefit of building automation networks can sometimes be expressed in money, e. g. saving energy costs, occasionally it is difficult when it is about increasing comfort or personal safety.

Typical universal building automation networks are open standards like LonWorks [EN149, DIE97], KNX [EN500, DIE00], and BACnet [ISO16, KRA05]. Other systems are specialized for certain applications like fire alarms or lighting (like the low-cost Digital Addressable Lighting Interface DALI [DAL06]) and might interface to universal building automation systems via gateways.

Different systems may be connected at the same level, e.g. field level (see Fig. 2-1), called horizontal integration. Or systems are considered to be self-contained and are connected via a common backbone network. That approach is called vertical integration and is going to become state of the art in modern BAC systems [SOU07]. The network management, however, does not get easier, the more gateways between different technologies are necessary. On the contrary, benefit regarding lifecycle costs and functionality is going to be maximized the more systems are combined [KAS05].

1.2 Functional Safety

Generally speaking, safety always deals with a reduction of risk to people. Additionally, as mentioned in [BUR92] risk in the context of safety results in immediate, direct harm. The standard IEC 61508 defines *safety* as "the absence of unacceptable risk of physical injury or damage to the health of people [...]" and risk as combination of the probability of a harm arising and the consequence (extent) of the harm [IEC61].

It has to be distinguished between electrical safety and functional safety. The first one deals with topics referring to the practical safeguarding of persons during installation, operation or maintenance of electric supply and communication lines and associated equipment [IEEC2]. *"Functional safety* is part of the overall safety that depends on a system or equipment operating correctly in response to its inputs." [IEC61-0] An over-temperature protection using a thermal sensor to de-energize a motor before it overheats, is an example of functional safety. However, providing some sort of insulation to withstand high temperature is not an instance of functional safety [IEC61-0]. Within this document writing about safety always means functional safety.

As mentioned before, safety is all about reducing the risk to people. The reason for risk is a hazard resulting from a hazardous failure. It is distinguished between systematic and stochastic failures resulting from stochastic or systematic faults. During development systematic faults are created, not intentionally, but accidentally. Typical systematic faults can be found for instance in the software design. Such faults can be avoided during development and detected during operation. Stochastic faults, however, can only be identified during operation and not avoided. Thus, the major tasks during development of a safety related system are *fault avoidance* and *fault control* subsumed by the word countermeasures in Fig. 1-1. Fault avoidance can be achieved by using development tools, structured and well written documents, or performing software code walkthroughs during software development. Fault control, i.e. detect and monitor faults, is realized by online self tests of the hardware or monitoring the execution of software.

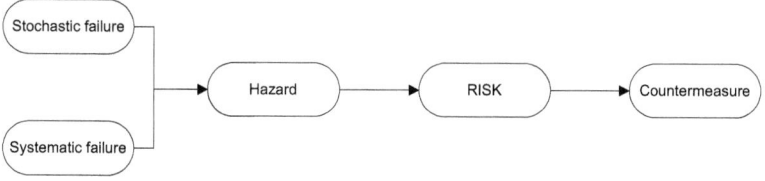

Fig. 1-1 Risk framework in the safety world [IEC61]

Systems that perform functions to reduce the amount of risk to an acceptable level and incorporate safety countermeasures are called safety related system. In such a system a failure is not necessarily critical. On the contrary, a safety critical system means a system where a single failure already causes a fatality [SMI04, p. 7] and is considered to be critical.

The first safety related systems were accomplished using conventional discrete electromechanical wiring, relays or contractor based interlocks. With the advent of microcomputers it was desired to use them in safety related systems in order to solve quite complex problems more simply and more economically. For that reason TUV Rheinland and TUV Bavaria wrote a handbook called 'Microcomputers in Safety Technique' [HOE86] that should help developers to design and build their system in such a way that it complies with all regulations. As a consequence, modern safety related systems consist of programmable and non-programmable hardware, or software, or both. They are created by applying measures to avoid systematic faults and include functionality to detect systematic and stochastic faults during operation.

One of the most important safety countermeasures to detect errors is the cyclic redundancy check (CRC). A CRC is a non-secure digest function for a data word which can be used to detect data corruption [KOO04]. From a mathematical point of view, a CRC is treating a binary data word as a polynomial with every polynomial coefficient being zero or one, and is performing polynomial division by a CRC polynomial where each coefficient is either zero or one. The rest of the division operation provides an error checking value either sent within a message or stored as data integrity check. The CRC calculation is based on an easy to implement and generic operation: the original data is placed bit by bit into a shift register and linked with the CRC polynomial by the exclusive OR operation. Consequently, performance of CRC calculation is in the range of tens of microseconds on an embedded device [PRE06, pp. 90].

Errors are detected by comparing the received CRC_{rcv} value in a message or the stored CRC_{sto} value of a data sequence with a CRC_{dyn} value calculated over the original data. An error is identified if the CRC_{dyn} is not equal to CRC_{rcv} or CRC_{sto}. Though, there is a low, but finite probability that a data corruption inverts a sufficient amount of bits in the right pattern and hence results in an undetectable error. I.e., $CRC_{dny} = CRC_{rvc}$, but multiple data bits are corrupted. The minimum number of bit inversions necessary to achieve an undetectable error is called hamming distance or hamming value.

CRC polynomials are distinguished by their hamming value. For instance, the 16 bit CRC polynomial CCITT-16 (the size of the CRC value is 2 byte) has a hamming distance of four. That is, all 1-bit, 2-bit and 3-bit errors are detected. If four bits are inverted in a single data word, they are not detected in 84 of all possible cases [KOO04]. Another example is the 15 bit CAN CRC polynomial with a hamming distance of six. It detects all 1-bit to 5-bit errors in a data sequence, but fails to reveal 4314 of the different 6-bit errors [KOO04]. It is noteworthy to say that a greater length of the CRC polynomial not necessarily results in a higher hamming value. However, a higher hamming value can only be reached with a larger CRC size.

The international standard IEC 61508 [IEC61] is the generic standard for functional safety of electrical, electronic and programmable electronic devices. It is based on the content of [HOE86]. It uses a risk based approach and an overall safety lifecycle model as a technical framework for the activities to ensure safety. The lifecycle model covers all safety activities from the initial concept to the final decommissioning. It specifies requirements for preventing failures and requirements for controlling failures, additionally techniques and measures necessary to achieve a level of safety.

It has spread enormously through most sectors of industry, such as process industry, IEC 61511 [IEC65] or railway, EN 50126 [EN501]. IEC 61508 can be applied on its own as a global template or as a basis to specify application specific standards [IEC61-0]. That is why it is the basis of all topics relating to safety discussed in the thesis.

Additional definitions used:

- *Fault* [IEE74]:
  (1) A defect in a hardware device or component; for example, a short circuit or broken wire
  (2) An incorrect step, process, or data definition in a computer program

- *Error* [IEE74]:
  The difference between a computed, observed or measured value or condition, and the true, specified, or theoretically correct value or condition; For

example, a difference of 30 meters between a computed result and the correct result.

- *Failure* [IEE74]:
  The inability of a system or component to perform its required functions within specified performance requirements

- *Fault tolerance* [IEC61-4]:
  The ability of a functional unit – consisting of hardware and/or software – to perform a given job despite the presence of faults or errors

- *Redundancy* [IEC61-4]:
  The presence of more than the minimal necessary means that enable a functional unit to perform a required function or to allow data to present information.

1.3 System Security

Within the thesis security is defined the following: "*Security* is concerned with the protection of assets from threats, where *threats* are categorized as the potential for abuse of protected assets" [IEC15]. *Assets* are described as information or resources to be protected by security countermeasures.

On the contrary to safety, security is about reduction of risk to information or resources coming from threats. Especially, security pays attention to those threats resulting from malicious or other intentional activities. In the context of security, risk enables or rises the ability of others to harm us [BUR92]. In the domain of security there are two main subdomains: network security or internet security, and system security or computer security [STA03, p. 2]. There are no clear boundaries between both subdomains. In [SCH00] good examples are given to get a feeling what system and network security is about. System security is concerned with security kernels, access control and strong cryptography; network security with firewalls, intrusion detection and auditing mechanism.

Typically, security related systems in building automation and control systems are striving for the following primary objectives [SCH03] subsumed by the acronym CIA and intending to protect assets from threats:

- *Confidentiality* – the property that ensures that information is accessible only to those authorized to have access [ISO17]
- *Integrity* – the property that safeguards the accuracy and completeness of information and processing methods [ISO17]
- *Availability* – the property that ensures that authorized users have access to information and associated assets when required [ISO17]

Secondary objectives also important are [DZU05]:
- *Authentication* – determination of the true identity of data or a user
- *Authorization*, also known as *access control* – preventing illegitimate users from accessing the system

Security services or functions derived from security objectives, i.e. countermeasures are applied to withstand an attack (threat action), reduce risk to the assets (Fig. 1-2). According to [RFC49], attacks are an assault on system security that derives from an intelligent threat. It is distinguished between *active* attacks and *passive* attacks. The first one wants to change assets or affect their operation. The other one tries to get or make use of assets without affecting the assets. Typical passive attacks are eavesdropping on, i.e. release of data content, or monitoring of transmissions, so called traffic analysis. Active attacks are for example masquerade that is, one entity pretends to be another; modification where some parts of data are changed [STA03, pp. 11]; or denial of service, i.e. prevention of authorized access to assets or delaying of operations [RFC49].

In addition, attacks are categorized in *inside* and *outside* attacks [RFC49]. An inside attack is an attack coming from an entity inside the security realm. I.e., an attack by an authorized entity that does not behave as expected. An outside attack is coming from outside the security realm initiated by an unauthorized entity.

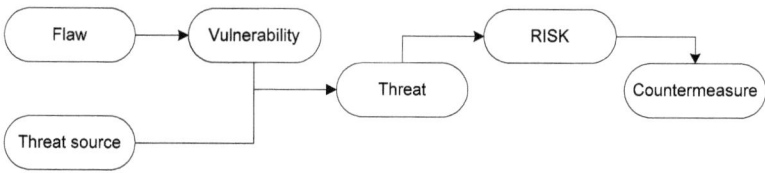

Fig. 1-2 Risk framework in the security world [STO02]

As shown in Fig. 1-2, threats that are exploited by a threat source – someone with the capability to exercise a vulnerability – result in an attack causing risk to assets. Vulnerabilities, in turn, are a result of flaws that can be deliberately exploited or unintentionally triggered. A flaw is a weakness in the implementation or design or an error such as a software bug.

Countermeasures, called security functions in the thesis, are implemented by different security measures. The most important and relevant for the understanding of the thesis are mentioned next. The strongest security measures are based on cryptographic methods [GOR00, p. 47]. It is noteworthy that implementing only cryptographic methods does not guarantee a defined level of security per se. Other activities discussed later in the thesis are required too.

Cryptography is the art and science of keeping data secure [SCH96]. A mathematical algorithm and a key are used to secure data. Whereas the mathematical algorithm is publically available, the keys are the secret. Securing data denotes encryption of a plaintext to a ciphertext and decryption of a ciphertext to a plaintext. Multiple so called cipher algorithms are available to encrypt and decrypt data. They can be divided into symmetric and asymmetric ciphers.

Symmetric ciphers such as 3-DES [NIS46-3] or AES [NIS19] use the same private key K_p for encryption and decryption of data. That is, entity A and entity B that share the same key K_p can communicate securely. Revealing the private key on entity A and transferring it to entity C results in a loss of security between entity A and B because Node C can read the ciphertext from entity A and B. Moreover, it can generate a valid ciphertext. Therefore, it is necessary to keep the private key secret.

There are two types of symmetric ciphers: stream ciphers and block ciphers. The first type encrypts a data stream one byte at a time. Examples of such ciphers are the autokeyed Vigenère cipher and the Vernam cipher [STA03, pp. 40]. On the contrary, block ciphers map a fixed size input block to a fix sized output block by means of a private key. Block sizes of 8 and 16 byte are used depending on the cipher. In addition, there are different ways of joining the single blocks. For example, the cipher block chaining mode (CBC) or the counter mode (CTR). In CBC mode the ciphertext of the last block $n-1$ is chained with the input plaintext block n

and ciphered afterwards. In CTR mode each input plaintext block is chained with a counter value and ciphered next. Block ciphers seem applicable to a wider range of applications than stream cipher and consequently are more popular [STA03, p. 64].

Asymmetric ciphers like [RSA78] or also called public ciphers use different keys for encryption and decryption. Due to the mathematical algorithm it is possible to make the key for encryption public. The key for decryption of ciphertext, however, must be kept secret. When entity A and entity B want to communicate securely, A encrypts the data with $K_{,B\text{-public}}$ and B decrypts the key with $K_{,B\text{-secret}}$. On the other hand, when B sends data to A is generates the ciphertext with key $K_{,A\text{-public}}$ and A decrypts the key with $K_{,A\text{-secret}}$. The advantage of asymmetric ciphers is that not every key must be kept secret. Loss of a public key does not result in breaching security. Size of asymmetric cipher keys compared to symmetric keys is much greater, though. Typically, private keys are 8 to 32 byte long whilst asymmetric keys are 64 to 256 byte long.

Ciphers can be used to encrypt and decrypt data of any length and grant its confidentiality. Additionally, ciphers are applied as basis to provide authenticity of data by means of a message authentication code (MAC). A MAC, or also known as cryptographic checksum, is a short piece of information and sometimes also called a tag. It is a function that gets a data sequence of variable length as input *M*, and generates an output *MAC* by using a secret key *K*.

$$MAC = C_K(M)$$

In case of having three specific properties as mentioned in [STA03, p. 327] to withstand attacks of an opponent who knows the function, a MAC is considered to be secure. First, it should be computational infeasible that an opponent constructs a new message *M'* that results in the same MAC that is the result of a message *M*. Second, it should thwart a brute-force attack, i.e. an attack with the goal to reveal the secret key. Third, the authentication function should not be weaker regarding certain portions or bits of the message than others. That is, it ought not include so called 'weak spots' susceptible to attacks.

Authentication with a MAC is based on the following principle: Entity A calculates a MAC_A over the message to be sent with the private key K_p and sends it to entity B. B also calculates the MAC_B with K_p by taking the received message as input. Authenticity is granted in case of $MAC_A = MAC_B$. An example of a MAC the CBC message authentication code (MAC) [NIS11]. A symmetric cipher in CBC mode is used where every block is taken as input to the following block. The length of the MAC is therefore equal to the block length.

In the field of security the Common Criteria (CC) (IEC 15408) are the international standard for information technology security. Products can be CC-certified and many organizations use the Common Criteria methodology. The Common Criteria have a mutual recognition agreement signed by more than a dozen of countries. I.e., products certified in one country are recognized in another [HER03, p. 1].

IEC 15408 addresses protection of information from unauthorized disclosure, modification, or loss of use, i.e. threats to confidentiality, integrity and availability. Especially, the standard concentrates on threats resulting from human activities. And Common Criteria are applicable to security measures realized in hardware, firmware or software [IEC15-1].

Due to their importance the Common Criteria are the basis of all topics related to system security in the thesis. However, not all parts of the CC are applicable for building automation and control systems such as privacy or non-repudiation because the CC are for IT security products.

2. Motivation and Possible Solution

The thesis is related to three fields of knowledge: functional safety, system security and building automation and control system (BACS). All of them were introduced in the previous chapter. However, why is safety and security in BACS important and why has the importance still been growing? In other words, what is the motivation for investigating safety together with security in BACS, not the personnel, but the technical one. And what is the problem regarding today's solutions. Second, a possible solution to the problem is presented: a common approach to safety and security where attention is paid to requirements from both sides during the whole system life.

2.1 Motivation and Problem Statement

A modern building automation and control system (BACS) is mostly accomplished with a fieldbus at the field level and used in a building to perform a given task in order to relieve human beings. Fieldbus stands for a network that connects sensors and actuators in the field, where field means some common processes [REI98, pp. 14]. Fieldbus systems substituted the discrete wiring among sensors and actuators, i.e. every connection among sensors and actuators is realized by a dedicated line. In the early years of building automation with fieldbus technology typical processes were heating, ventilation and air-conditioning (HVAC). Later on lighting and shading processes have been integrated. The BACS was completely isolated without any possibility of accessing it from the outside. Therefore, the system was not considered to be security critical. And a BACS was safety critical neither. In safety critical environments sensors, actuators and logic elements had to be wired discretely.

In the last years the field of application of BACS has been extended (e.g. fire alarm or intrusion detection systems) to allow improvements in building control and cost reduction [GRA06]. Consequently, more sophisticated and integrated services are necessary. Previously independent and isolated service domains must be integrated [SOU07]. Systems with an enormous amount of nodes are becoming more likely. Additionally, the wireless technology is becoming popular in BACS [REI07]. It partly replaces the physical bus system. All facts mentioned make new demands on a BACS and require new properties. Two important properties are safety and security, often called quality properties of a system in the field of software engineering [FIR03]. Quality properties result in supplementary requirements [POO05]. The intention of such requirements is to support primary requirements. Therefore the supplementary requirements put constraints on how primary functionality is implemented. Mentioned later, but for the sake of understanding subsequent chapters outlined already at the beginning, in the following safety and security requirements are not considered to be supplementary or to be an additional quality attribute. They are the most important requirements in the common approach.

Today's BAC systems are systems with an enormous amount of nodes, even more than 10000 due to the integration of various processes. Typically, nodes are grouped in subsystems at the field level as shown in Fig. 2-1. Sensors and actuators are connected to the nodes and they are interacting with the environment. At the field level low bandwidth and cost effective systems are used. Subsystems are connected via gateways over the backbone network. Such networks are private and high bandwidth networks and are often using standard IT technology. They are connecting the different subsystems with network management devices and public networks like the Internet.

Compared to automotive systems, BAC systems are quite dynamic and are subject to changes or reconfigurations. Just think of how often employees in an office building have to move and for example light control has to be rearranged – either network topology or parameters have to be changed. Consequently, sophisticated tools to manage the system are required. Management includes jobs related to installation, commissioning, and maintenance or decommissioning. Since tasks should be managed even among subsystems, the network management device running the tools resides at the backbone level. For control reasons such tools also give the user the possibility to access the network remotely via Internet. At that

Motivation and Possible Solution

level access to all subsystems results in the possibility to monitor and control the BACS in a centralized way. By providing a unified visualization scheme to an operator, abnormal and faulty conditions can be detected, localized and corrected easily at an early stage. Furthermore, direct access to BACS data eases data acquisition [KAS05].

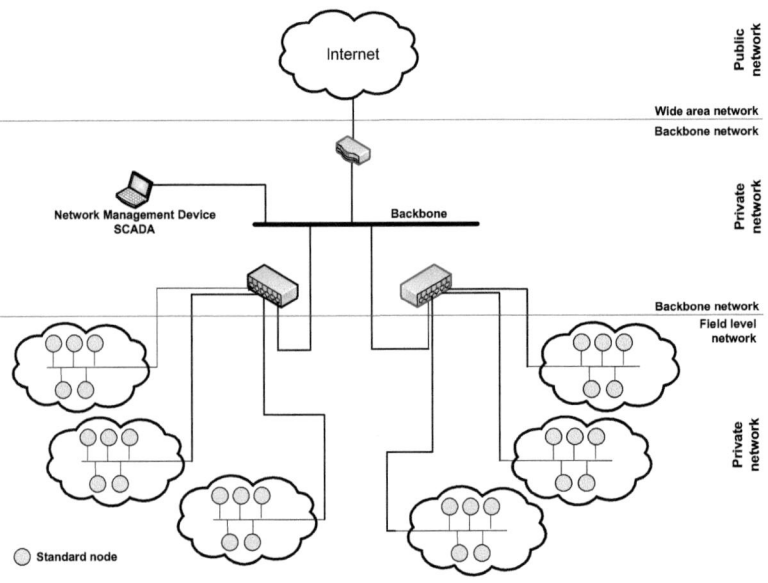

Fig. 2-1 BACS architecture [KAS05]

Additionally, more and more wireless technology at the field level is going to be employed in automation systems in general. Wireless technology reduces installation costs because wiring of nodes is not necessary. Moreover, installation effort and maintenance costs of the physical infrastructure are minimized compared to wired systems. For example, a wireless extension to KNX/EIB is presented in [REI07] using IEEE 802.15.4 [IEE80]. The ZigBee specification – based on IEEE 802.15.4 – for wireless sensor networks has already been used in oil and gas industry as a cost efficient means to enable a whole new range of applications [PET07]. It is a robust network and supports low data rate monitoring and control applications. In the mesh network topology it can be implemented with a very large number of nodes. Consequently, applying wireless sensor networks in BACS is also a topic. Such an approach is presented in [MAH03]. Wireless ad-hoc networks with a limited range of about some tens of meters are integrated into an automation system. As a result a broad range of new services and an increasing of the flexibility of a automation system is possible. In [ÖST07] another approach is presented that integrates wireless sensor networks in BACS: BACnet [ISO16] is used on top of a wireless sensor network.

Facing the innovations in BAC systems, the severity of security problems has been increasing dramatically, in terms of the number of problems but also their consequences. The BACS cannot be considered an isolated island any more, i.e. without any access from the outside and wired node to node communication inside the network. Interconnection of subsystems over a backbone network such as an IP-based LAN for enabling process monitoring, results in the possibility of attacks from *inside* of the system [REY05]. Moreover, attacks from *outside* the BACS are likely if the backbone network is further connected to a public network like the internet. Finally, employing wireless technology in particular and open media in general tighten the security problem.

BAC systems are intended to be used in more and more fields of application, including safety critical environments like hospitals and safety critical services, respectively. Additionally, the demand on personal safety in general in our society is constantly growing and lowers the level of risk accepted to life of people. That fact has been taken into considerations by the national and European legislation.

A typical safety critical service is a fire detection service. It is obvious that failures in a fire detection system or failures in an application in a hospital can have severe consequences such as human injury or even death. So the risk resulting from critical stochastic and systematic failures must be reduced. In other words, the safety integrity (i.e. reliability with respect to catastrophic failures [KOP97, p. 10] assuming that safety is a subset of reliability – one of various definitions of the relationship between safety and reliability [GER02]) has to be reasonable high. As pointed out in subchapter 1.2, a system that incorporates safety techniques to reduce risk is called safety related. Strict requirements given by international standards like IEC 61508 have to be met by a safety related BACS. Requirements comprise the design, realization, deployment and maintenance phase of a system. And there are requirements that specify the way of developing and what to develop. Success of a product is inevitably linked to meet such requirements.

Today's BACS guard against some security problems, depending on fieldbus technology and type of installation. Safeguards vary in terms of supported security features and kind of implementation. For example, LonWorks [EN149] incorporates an integrity service, standard KNX [EN500] not. The integrity service in LonWorks is based on an undisclosed cryptographical algorithm, BACnet [ISO16] uses the publicly available advanced encryption standard (AES) algorithm [NIS19]. A survey on the three most common BACS regarding their security features can be found in chapter 3. Additionally, on the contrary to industrial automation systems safety features are not included in standard BAC systems. However, efforts are made to make LonWorks safe [NOV07, HER08]. The basic idea is to enhance the standard system with safety features on application level.

To sum up the aforementioned, it has to be stated that there are safety and security requirements on a modern BACS differing in the degree of rigor. Some of the BACS are satisfying a number of security requirements, a single one presented in [NOV07, HER08] is going to meet a few security requirements *and* specified safety requirements. The problem, still remaining unsolved, is that safety and security are examined independently: safety and security features are developed and integrated without paying attention to their dependencies. Safety related systems most likely incorporate security flaws and consequently will not withstand intentional attacks from the inside or outside. In contrast, security threats, e.g. breaching integrity of hard- or software, will have safety consequences: a (critical) failure occurs, leading to a hazardous event.

A step further on making BAC systems more safe and secure is to examine them in terms of safety *and* security. Especially, the dependencies between them are worth being investigated: the commonalities and contradictions. A common approach to safety and security in BACS shows in which situations they are similar or even identical, and therefore effort in development can be reduced. Commonalities can be found in the context of technical objectives or non-functional measures like methods to assess risk. Pointing out contradictions is another topic to be taken into account in the common approach. Of course, a BACS will never be totally safe and totally secure – a trade-off is necessary what feature weights more in a defined context. However, a list with contradictions forces to think of the intention, the environment of the BACS and so on. Afterwards the field of application is clear and either safety or security is preferred.

2.2 Possible Solution of Common Approach

The common approach presents a way of how to deal with safety and security issues as well as how to build a safe and secure BACS. Therefore, the challenge is to specify a way of

1. how to integrate safety and security, i.e. concept and methodology and
2. how to develop and use such a building automation and control system (BACS), i.e. 'development-use' model.

Additionally, it must meet some distinct design requirements because its success is without doubt linked to the acceptance of safety experts and security practitioners, and BACS developers and integrators. Hence, the common approach shall be based on standard methodology and shall use standard terms known in the safety and security society, respectively. In the safety domain it is an established practice [BAT96, HAM91, IEC61] to use a lifecycle model as 'development-use' model. Within the thesis lifecycle model is used as generic term for every procedure starting with a product's conception and ending with its disposal. Or, as mentioned in [MOL02] a lifecycle model specifies a logical activity flow of a project. Consequently, the common approach shall cover all stages of the lifecycle of a system. As stated in [BUR92] safety and security are subject to different legislations and standards with regard to the development, use and assessment. Thus, another requirement is that the common approach is accepted by the relevant bodies and therefore shall adhere to the requirements given by international standards. Finally, systems built in accordance with the common approach should be comparable to each other. So it is required that one or more levels are specified giving information on the degree of safety and security, respectively.

Referring to the aforementioned first objective, a common approach has to specify a way of how to integrate safety and security. As mentioned in [EAM99], the word integrate can mean *unifying* safety and security. Alternatively, it can stand for *harmonizing* safety and security. While unifying implies creating a new concept and methodology, a harmonizing approach intends to use standard concepts and methodologies from both disciplines and shows how safety and security interact. That is the way how the common approach presented in the thesis looks like since it meets the design requirement: acceptance of safety, security and BACS people. Unification of safety and security attributes together with reliability and maintainability is an approach called dependability [LAP92].

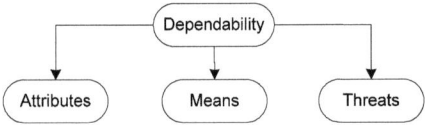

Fig. 2-2 The dependability tree

According to [IEE98] dependability is defined as follows: "Trustworthiness of a computer system such that reliance can be justifiably placed on the service it delivers. Reliability, availability, and maintainability are aspects of *dependability*." Dependability is a unifying concept and consists of three parts: the threats to, the attributes of and the means by which dependability is reached as shown in Fig. 2-2 [AVI04].

As presented in Fig. 2-2, threats to a system can results from three different reasons (fault, error, failure). Risk coming from threats can be lowered by applying different means like fault prevention, fault tolerance, fault removal and fault forecast. These means or techniques are used in order to reduce the probability of endangering one or more dependability attributes of a system. According to [AVI04] attributes are defined as follows.

- Availability: Readiness for correct service
- Reliability: Continuity of correct service
- Safety: Absence of catastrophic consequences on the user(s) and the environment
- Confidentiality: Absence of unauthorized disclosure of information
- Integrity: Absence of improper system state alterations
- Maintainability: Ability to undergo repairs and modifications

Whereas safety is an explicit attribute of dependability and its definition is similar in content to the one presented in subchapter 1.2, security is not mentioned explicitly. However, the attributes of security as mentioned in subchapter 1.3 are integrated into the concept. The definition of integrity and availability differs, though. In the security context the attribute availability and integrity is linked to the topic of authorization. With regard to dependability security is the concurrent existence of the three attributes confidentiality, integrity and availability.

In short, safety and security deal with the avoidance of a specific class of failure (hazardous failures, threats, vulnerabilities). Dependability widens the scope and means the prevention of any kind of failure. Therefore reliability is added as an attribute and availability is defined in a broader context. And the concept redefines standard terms of domains like security. As a consequence, the concept of dependability is not suitable for a common approach to functional safety and system security. Especially, security practitioners must acquaint themselves with a new terminology and concept.

Type A standard	Generic standard
	IEC 61508 for functional safety or IEC 15408 for IT security
Type B standard	Domain specific standard
	Railway: EN 50126; Process industry: IEC 61511
Type C standard	Application specific standard
	Railway: EN 50128

Fig. 2-3 Hierarchy of standards

A second way to integrate safety and security is to harmonize both disciplines. The intention of the harmonizing approach is that safety experts apply the safety related concept and methodology and security practitioners the security related one. Such a way is reasonable since special techniques in the different domains evolved and are adapted to the individual needs. Using techniques from safety and security also gives the possibility to see what can be borrowed from the other discipline. Furthermore, applying standard techniques in the safety and security domain increase the possibility of revealing the dependencies, communalities and conflicts, clearly. The challenge of the harmonizing approach is to develop a rule based conflict resolution approach. That forces the safety experts and security practitioners to think of the respective other discipline and to interact with each other. It finally results in a better understanding of the BACS.

Fig. 2-3 [WRA07, p. 270] gives an overview of the hierarchy of standards. It is a three tier hierarchy with generic standards at the top. Type A standards include general term definitions and basic procedures used in a specific area, such as functional safety (IEC 61508) or IT security (IEC 15408). Type B standards correspond to a certain domain, such as railway, automotive or process industry. They cover particular aspects of the different domains, but inherit the basics of a generic standard. At the bottom type C standards are located. That type of standard is specialized to give requirements for a particular application, e.g. safety rules for installation of lifts (EN 81) or software for railway control and protection systems (EN 50128). In the field of BAC systems no standard relating to safety or security has been available yet, neither of type C nor type B. Therefore as mentioned already in subchapter 1.2 and 1.3 two type A standards for safety (IEC 61508) and security (IEC 15408) are chosen as reference for concept and methodology in the respective discipline.

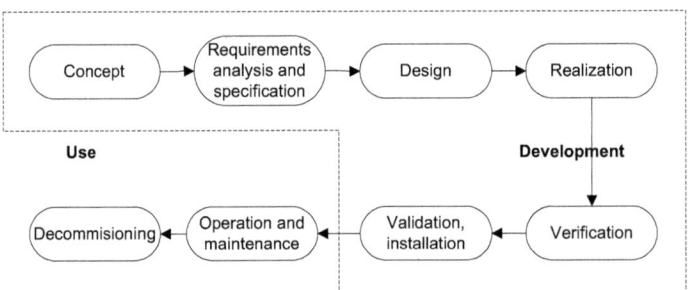

Fig. 2-4 Generic lifecycle

The 'development-use' model, the second challenge, is realized by a lifecycle model because it is a structured and systematic model covering the development and use of a system. Typically, as shown in Fig. 2-4, a lifecycle starts with the concept phase including a definition of the scope, the purpose and examination of the environment. Next, a requirements analysis is performed and a specification is set up. It includes functional, performance, usability, reliability, supportability or design-constraints requirements. After that, a design or architecture of the system is created that is realized in a further step. Subsequently, the built product is verified. *Verification* is the process of evaluating a system to determine if the products of a given development phase satisfy the conditions imposed at the start of that phase [IEE74]. In other words, it is asked, 'Are we building the product right?' Following the verification process, the system is installed and validated. *Validation* is the process of evaluating a system during or at the end of the development process to find out whether it satisfies specified requirements [IEE74]. Validating a product is associated with the question, 'Are we building the right product?' In the use-phase, the system is in operation and has to be maintained. At the end the system is decommissioned.

As already outlined shortly, a lifecycle approach has become 'best practice' in the safety domain. There has been a common understanding that activities such as fault avoidance and fault control must be applied at the different stages of the lifecycle. Hence, the number of systematic failures can be reduced. Often safety assessment work has been confined to assessing whether the proposed architecture meets the target failure probabilities [SMI04, p. 11]. Less attention was paid to the installation, maintenance and disposal phase [WRA07, p. 1].

Similar approaches, albeit less detailed and accepted, have been development in the security domain. In [MCG06, pp. 27] it is outlined that building any type of software securely is only possible if security issues are considered during all phases of the lifecycle. Hence, seven so called touchpoints (a set of best practices) are introduced, each of them applicable to a different lifecycle phase. [AME05] also highlights that security related issues in general are present during the different phases of a lifecycle. In [LIP04] the so called 'trustworthy computing security development lifecycle' is discussed. It was developed by Microsoft and consists of a set of high-level principles presented in chapter 5.2. Although the lifecycle is implemented to develop IT software, the activities during the different lifecycle phases are the same for embedded software. In general, the trend to ensure security during the various stages of a product life is clearly perceptible. Its importance is growing due to the increasing complexity and connectivity of security critical systems.

2.3 Scope of the Thesis

In conclusion, a solution to the problem of safety and security in BAC systems is a common approach harmonizing safety and security discipline. Thereby, both disciplines remain independent and use the respective concept and methodology where applicable. Attention is paid to the dependencies of both disciplines and therefore *new additional* activities such as a concept to resolve conflicts are proposed in the following. It is shown how to benefit from the commonalities. Topics referring to safety are according to IEC 61508, security related are in accordance with IEC 15408. The 'development-use' model is a lifecycle model that gives requirements for the different lifecycle phases of the BACS. The target audience of the common approach is the developer, operator and maintainer of BAC systems. Topics relating to the acquisition of a project or, generally, procurement activities like independent cost estimation or contract issues are not part of the common approach.

The common approach is applicable to create a new safe-secure BACS or to enhance a standard BACS with new features and widen the field of application. Discussion of common approach in the thesis focuses on the development and use of an *existing* BACS. Due to economic reasons that will be the case for almost all further developments in the field of general purpose BAC systems.

Important to mention is that the common approach can be the basis of standardization. That is why international standards are taken as reference for the respective disciplines. Nevertheless, this thesis does not cover all aspects required for a standard. The work presented by the author subsequently intends to give an example how a common approach may look like and how to handle it when building up a safe and secure BACS. As much information is given to understand the basic ideas of the approach.

Although an approach to a system lifecycle is presented, it is beyond the scope of the thesis to give examples of how to develop and use the *complete* BACS including nodes, gateways, installation and management tools, management devices and so on. Within the thesis the focus of attention is on the field level of a BACS (Fig. 2-1), especially on the *node* and its environment, the hardware in general and the software in particular. Other entities and issues are discussed only in such detail necessary to understand the context presented.

3. Safety and Security in Today's Automation Systems

The intention of fieldbus systems used at the field level of an automation system has been to replace discrete wiring of sensors and actuators as mentioned in subchapter 2.1. As a consequence, the traditional services heating, ventilation and air-conditioning (HVAC) in BACS became more flexible and more popular accordingly. These services are neither safety nor security critical. That is the reason why today's BACS do not incorporate sufficient security features. Moreover, they are not featured with safety at all although some effort is done to enhance LonWorks with safety features [NOV07].

In the following the three universal building automation systems are examined also regarding their security features. More general information is conveyed on LonWorks because the building automation system is used in the use case presented in chapter 8. The result of the security investigation is giving an additional motivation to pay attention to the topic security in BACS. Additionally, some safety related automation systems are analyzed to show how safety features can be integrated into an automation system.

3.1 BACnet

In 1987 the American Society of Heating, Refrigerating and Air-Conditioning (ASHRAE) started with the development of a protocol that addresses the needs of building automation and control systems of various sizes and types. In 1995 the development of BACnet was finally completed and it was published as ANSI/ASHRAE Standard 135-1995. At the moment the current version of the standard is ANSI/ASHRAE Standard 135-2004. Additionally, addenda are made to the standard in order to consider new needs coming from the market. Addendum *a* to *f* are approved for publication and addendum *g* is now available for trial implementation. In the year 2003 BACnet was also adopted as international standard, ISO standard [ISO16]. The goal of standardization has been to achieve interoperability in BACS.

BACnet is a vendor independent data transmission protocol for open communication in BACS. It specifies a layer 3 and layer 7 of the OSI reference model [ISO74; KRA05, pp. 103]. BACnet does not determine the underlying layers 1 and 2. However, it specifies five different network types differing in performance and costs that are supported such as Ethernet or LonTalk. In 1999 BACnet/IP was introduced to also make use of the Internet protocol. Because of the aforementioned network types physical media like twisted pair or fiber optic can be used.

BACnet is based on an object model that represents the functionality of the BACS. An object summarizes data elements that correspond to a particular function. Each object consists of a number of properties. E.g., an analogue output object includes the property 'Present_Value' or 'Description'. Each device can have none, one or many objects with the exception of the 'Device' object. Each device must have one and only one 'Device' object. It is used in the BACS to identify and control multiple characteristics of the device. Especially, it keeps a list of all other objects existing on the device.

BACnet does not mandate any specific hardware, but it specifies five device types based on a device profile. In other words, requirements are given how a BACnet device has to look like. Typical device types are the BACnet operator workstations (B-OWS), a management equipment, or the BACnet advanced application controller (B-AAC), a configurable device, or the BACnet smart actuator (B-SA) or sensor (B-SS) [KRA05, pp. 123].

In contrast to the following BACS, BACnet incorporates many security features to ensure security objectives like authentication, confidentiality and integrity. The security architecture relies on the data encryption standard (DES) [NIS46-2] crypto algorithm and a central trusted key server [SCH03]. Some topics relevant for a defined level of security are not addressed in BACnet: the initial key distribution (keys used to secure device and key server communication), storage of private keys on a device or the generation of keys. Additionally, the security approach incorporates some weaknesses such as the central key server (single point of failure) or the use of DES (not considered to be secure enough any more due to the short key size and increasing computational power [RFC47]).

Since the original security mechanisms in BACnet, based on the old Data Encryption Standard (DES), have been rendered insecure by advances in computer technology, the BACnet Network Security Working Group has developed replacement mechanisms based on the newer Advanced Encryption Standard (AES) [NIS19] published in addendum *g* to ANSI/ASHRAE standard 135-2004. An additional advantage of AES is that it is simple enough that all BACnet can be secured, which would have been difficult and computational expensive with the computation heavy DES.

3.2 KNX/EIB

The European Installation Bus (EIB) is a fieldbus designed for home and building automation. In 1990 the EIBA (EIB Association) was founded that maintained the open specification. In the year 2002 EIB was merged with Batibus and European Home System (EHS) to form the new KNX standard [KNX04]. The standard seeks to combine the best features of the three systems mentioned before. The goal is to create a single European home and building electronic system (HBES) standard. Nowadays, KNX is maintained by the Konnex Association and EIB exists unchanged as a set of profiles within KNX, called KNX/EIB.

The KNX/EIB protocol stack consists of layer 1-4 and layer 7. The layer 5 and 6 are not implemented [DIE00, p. 56]. It supports physical media like twisted pair or powerline. Moreover, there is an extension called EIBnet/IP available that gives the opportunity to use an IP based medium as transport channel.

The KNX/EIB communication model is based on a shared variable model. Network-visible variables of a node are called group objects. They can be readable, writeable or both. Objects can be grouped and the group is assigned a unique group address. The address is used to handle the network traffic. Additionally, system management objects are implemented to access network management data like binding information. And application interface objects can be provided relating to the intended behavior of the application.

The KNX specification also includes standard hardware components. The most important part of a component is the bus coupling unit (BCU). It consists of a microcontroller (MC68HC05 family) and a transceiver which makes access to the bus possible. The complete protocol stack and an application environment are implemented on the unit. The BCU can host simple application programs. So called application modules like a thermostat can be connected to the BCU via an external interface

KNX/EIB only offers security on a rudimentary scale. The application layer provides password based services to control access to the memory of the node and its object properties. Even worse, the passwords are sent in plaintext to the node. Because of the lack of security attempts have been made to enhance KNX/EIB so that it grants a medium level of security.

One of the attempts is called EIBsec [GRA05, pp. 132, GRA06]. It relies on a distributed security solution to avoid a single point of failure. EIBsec supports data confidentiality and integrity, authentication of both communication participants, protection of management and process data, and mechanism for initial key distribution and for key management. The advanced encryption standard (AES) [NIS19] is applied for granting the security objectives.

Each network segment contains a security related device, the advanced coupler unit (ACU). The ACU is a security enhanced line or backbone coupler that acts as a key server. It is responsible for distribution and generation of keys. In EIBsec different types of keys are specified like the session key for device to device communication, group key for multicast messages or the node key and its companion the dynamic node key to retrieve other keys from the ACU in a secure way.

Initial key distribution is solved quite easily. The lower part of the key is sent with one, the higher part of the message with another message. To check if the remote entity is allowed to change the key a password mechanism is used. Since the key is sent in plaintext such a way of initial key distribution is only secure if unauthorized access to the network is not possible. Otherwise, the keys must be uploaded to the device manually. Secure storage of the uploaded keys is not guaranteed in the approach because physical security is not part of EIBsec – a clear weakness of the proposed solution.

3.3 LonWorks

The company Echelon developed LonWorks, an event triggered control network system, in 1991/92. The intention was to cover about 80% of BACS application [DIE97, p. 23]. The system consists of the LonTalk communication protocol, a dedicated controller (Neuron Chip [MOT97] or LC3020 [LOY05]) and a network management tool. The LonTalk protocol is standardized in ANSI/EIA-709 in America and in EN 14908-1 in Europe. In 1994 the LonMark Interoperability Association (today called LonMark International) was founded which specifies guidelines for interoperable devices.

The LonTalk protocol incorporates all 7 layers of the OSI reference model and supports a variety of channels: twisted-pair, powerline or fiber optic. A very popular channel in building automation is the free topology twisted pair (TP/FT-10) [KAS05]. Also IP tunneling is possible, called LonWorks/IP and standardized in ANSI/EIA-852 in America.

The communication in LonWorks is possible by means of network variables or explicit messages. A network variable is a data item that an application on Device A expects to get from Device B on a network (an input network variable) or expects to make available to Device B on a network (an output network variable). Network variables are used for operational data such as temperatures, or pressures and are limited to 31 byte. A lot of NV are specified for interoperability purpose and called standard network variable type (SNVT). Network variables of the same type, but opposite direction can be connected – they are logically connected by performing a binding. Moreover, explicit messages are used if messages larger than 31 byte must be sent or a request/response service is desired [DIE97, pp. 183].

As already mentioned, there are two chips available that can be used as network nodes: the Neuron Chip or the LC3020. The first one is integrated if just small applications have to be executed on the node. They are identified in the network by an unique device ID, in case of installing a Neuron Chip referred to as Neuron ID. Each chip provides input and outputs where sensors or actuators are plugged in. Depending on the channel, the nodes are equipped with different transceivers.

Although LonWorks was published rather late compared to other fieldbus systems, security issues have also been neglected. LonWorks only offers authentication services that are implemented at layer 4 and 5 of the OSI reference model. There is no possibility to encrypt data and access control is handled on a per node basis.

Authentication is realized by a challenge response mechanism. Node A (writer) send message to Node B (reader) where the authentication bit is set, i.e. Node B expects an authentication of Node A. The reader generates a random number and returns it to Node A. In addition, it generates a one way transformation of the created random number and the data in the message using its private authentication key. The result is a 64 bit hash value. Node A does the same and sends its hash value to Node B. Finally, the reader compares the values and the result (successful or failed) is given to the application layer. That is, the application decides how to interpret the result.

The cryptographic algorithm used to as one way transformation function is not publically available. Therefore, it must be considered to be insecure because it opposes Kerckhoff's principle [KER83]: All algorithms must be public; only the keys are secret. Keeping the algorithm secret is referred to as security by obscurity which never works [TAN03, p. 726]. The authentication key is 48 bit long and it is assumed that it is not strong enough [SCH03]. In the end, only a single authentication key can be stored on a node. If a group of nodes use authentication service, all of them have to share the same key. Consequently, authenticity of a designated node cannot be verified any more. It can only be ensured that the node belongs to the group.

Because of the weaknesses regarding security, in [SCH03] an approach is presented that increases the level of security. The simple idea is to equip nodes with a smartcard and to integrate security services on top of the protocol layer (above application layer). The smartcard is a security token and a tamper proof device, i.e. data located on the card are considered to be secure. All cryptographic operations are performed and the private keys are stored on the smartcard. A security application cares for transferring sensor and actuator data to the smartcard and for reading it back. As a consequence, authenticity, integrity and confidentiality of data sent over the network can be guaranteed. Confidentiality and authenticity of data in the memory on the node is not ensured by the approach. By means of network management tools, the values can be written and read. In other words, transmission security, but not security of data on the node is tackled by the approach.

3.4 Safety Related Automation Systems

Safety related automation systems are accomplished by enhancing the standard protocol and/or adapting the hardware of the standard nodes. Such systems have to be implemented in a way so that systematic failures and stochastic failures are detected during the operation resulting from node or network faults. In the following three safety related automation systems out of a great amount of safe automation systems are presented to give an overview of common safety mechanisms.

The *CAN* bus was developed in the mid 1980 by the company BOSCH for the automotive sector. It specifies a layer 1 and 2 as well as a layer 7 called CANopen of the ISO reference model. The CAN fieldbus was made safe by extending the CANopen protocol with safety features. The protocol is referred to as *CANopen Safety* [REI01, pp. 73; WRA07, pp. 140]. That is, no safety layer above layer 7 was developed since sensors and actuators are directly connected. And the actuator must meet defined safety requirements.

Safety of CAN relies on the fault detection mechanism of standard CAN. Additionally, to increase integrity and reduce residual failure probability messages are sent twice and the second one is inverted. The two standard messages comprise a single safe message. To distinguish safety and non-safety related messages, the identifier range in the standard message was extended. Finally, watchdog functionality is integrated to detect if a safe message part or a complete safe message was lost.

CANopen Safety meets safety requirements of safety integrity level (SIL) 3 (refer to subchapter 4.1 for the details) given by the international standard IEC 61508 [IEC61]. Since the protocol enhancement was not sufficient to meet the desired safety level, a hardware architecture with two channels was chosen. In other words, a safe node consists of a single transceiver, two CAN controllers and two additional safety chips. The safety chips are cross-checking the received data independently and ensure that the data received has not been altered during transfer.

In 1999 the first machine was put into operation whose safety functionality was realized by an open fieldbus system meeting requirements of category 4 of EN 954-1 [EN954-1]. It is called *SafetyBUS p* [REI01, pp. 175] and based on the

CAN protocol layer 1 and 2. Safety features are incorporated into the application layer (layer 7).

In contrast to CANopen Safety, SafetyBUS p specifies a safety message format. It is embedded into the payload field of the standard CAN message: a one byte header including the message type and a sequence number to verify the loss of messages, a one byte target address to identify if the message has been chosen for the node, four byte payload and a 2 byte CRC to ensure the integrity of the safety related message. Moreover, acknowledgements are sent by returning the received message inverted to the sender to detect corruption, insertion of messages and loss of messages. The last mentioned fault can be detected in case of using a watchdog that is triggered if the acknowledgement is not received within a predefined time frame. Safety and non-safety related messages can be distinguished by a special class of identifiers in the standard CAN message format (same mechanism used in CANopen Safety).

Safety is further supported by dedicated hardware architecture of the node. A two channel architecture is used that consists of a single transceiver and CAN controller, and two safety chips. The chips are working independently and are cross-checking received messages. Such an approach decreases the residual failure probability because only if both channels come to the same result, the message payload is valid, i.e. integrity is granted.

In 1999 another safety related system was published called *PROFIsafe*. It is an extension to standard *PROFIBUS* [REI01, pp. 155]. The protocol of PROFIBUS includes layer 1, 2 and 7 of the OSI reference model. It is equipped with a number of safety features to meet requirements of safety integrity level 3 (SIL) specified in IEC 61508.

PROFIsafe is based on the 'black channel' concept [WRA07, pp. 132], i.e. the standard equipment is not considered in the safety assessment, but faults resulting from the channel must be detected. Safety features to detect such faults are summarized in a dedicated safety layer above layer 7. Additionally, an interface to the safety layer is available to provide the safety functionality to the application programmer in a convenient way. As it is done in SafetyBUS p, PROFIsafe uses a safety message format that is embedded into the payload of standard messages. It includes a status byte to synchronize the status between host and slave, a sequence number and a 2 byte CRC. In addition, authentication of sender and receiver is provided by a password unique for every master and slave. And a watchdog function is integrated to detect a delay and loss of messages.

Whilst the two aforementioned safety related automation systems are based on a two channel hardware architecture, PROFIsafe only uses a single architecture. Put another way, the standard hardware is not altered, just the firmware of the nodes is enhanced with the safety functionality.

To sum up, the three examples mentioned before show that there are basic mechanisms applied to include safety functionality: additional safe message format embedded into the standard protocol, or watchdog functionality, CRCs or a two channel hardware architecture. Safety functions are located in layer 7 or in dedicated safety layer above the layer 7. Also noteworthy to outline that most safety related automation system adhere to requirements of SIL 3 of the IEC 61508 standard – category 4 is equivalent to SIL 3 with regard to the rigor of the safety requirements [WRA07, p. 72].

4. International Standards

A requirement to be met by the common approach in general is that it should be widely accepted in the safety, security and BACS community. Thus, all topics referring to lifecycle issues are based on international standards in order not to reinvent the wheel. Safety related topics in the common approach are covered by IEC 61508 whereas IEC 15408 or also known as Common Criteria comprises all security related issues.

IEC 61508 is chosen because it is a generic standard, i.e. not application specific, and therefore applicable to all applications. As mentioned in [IEC61-0], its intention is to be used as standalone standard or as a basis of other standards. It includes different levels that can be used to distinguish systems. Finally, it specifies a safety lifecycle model and activities to guarantee a certain degree of safety quality.

The Common Criteria (IEC 15408) cover all aspects of IT security and allow for comparing different systems by introducing evaluation assurance levels (EAL). Moreover, they specify activities for many lifecycle stages that help to assure a level of security quality. Finally, they also incorporate a way of deriving security functions. In short, these attributes are the reason that the Common Criteria are the preferred choice.

4.1 Safety and IEC 61508

The international standard IEC 61508 [IEC61] standardizes a lifecycle model for creating a safety related systems. It specifies requirements for every stage of the life of a system to avoid faults during the design and to control faults during operation. It aims at providing a technical sound, system based and risk based approach for determining the necessary performance of safety related systems. In addition, it provides a means for users and regulators to gain confidence when using computer based technology [IEC61-0].

Safety related systems are developed to reduce the inherent risk of the Equipment Under Control (EUC) below the maximum tolerable risk by applying a variety of measures: functional ones like online tests or non-functional ones as part of the functional safety management [IEC61-7]. The EUC, for example, corresponds with the building automation and control system (BACS) or an entity of the BACS like a node. The amount and kind of measures incorporated in a safety related system are always specified on account of hazards and their associated risks. As a result, developing a safety related system always requires a hazard and risk analysis of the EUC. It consists of a specification of hazards causing a dangerous situation, a description of the reason of the hazards and an identification of risks associated with the different hazards.

Safety requirements describing how to handle hazards in a safe way are derived from the hazard and risk analysis. Safety requirements define the behavior of the safety functions performed by the safety related system. Beside safety requirements there are also safety integrity requirements, i.e. performance requirements for the safety functions, necessary to be defined in order to achieve functional safety with a safety related system. Safety integrity requirements specify the possibility of a safety function being performed according to expectation. Safety integrity requirements are derived from the risk assessment where the risk of every hazard is determined.

Table 4-1. Safety integrity level (IEC 61508)

Safety integrity level (SIL)	High demand or continuous mode (Failure probability per hour)
4	$\geq 10^{-9}$ to $< 10^{-8}$
3	$\geq 10^{-8}$ to $< 10^{-7}$
2	$\geq 10^{-7}$ to $< 10^{-6}$
1	$\geq 10^{-6}$ to $< 10^{-5}$

The performance of the safety functions is categorized by four safety integrity levels (SIL) defined in IEC 61508. Safety integrity level 1 (SIL 1) is the lowest and safety integrity level 4 (SIL 4) is the highest level. Each level corresponds with a specific failure probability per hour (see Table 4-1). The value of the failure probability specifies the probability of a dangerous failure per hour. On account of the safety integrity level the likelihood for successfully performing the safety functions is defined. The lower the likelihood of dangerous failures the higher the performance of the safety functions must be and the more thorough are the safety integrity requirements.

After specifying the safety functions and the safety integrity level, designing a safety related system additionally requires a consideration of the deployed hardware on which the safety functions are executed. The maximum safety integrity level is restricted because of the hardware fault tolerance (see Table 4-2 for an explanation) and the safe failure fraction (SFF). The SFF specifies the quantity of failures that do not result in a dangerous situation. That is, the higher the SFF the more failures are detected and the less *dangerous* failures are undetected.

Generally, there are two types of failures possible: stochastic (random) and systematic failures resulting from stochastic and systematic faults, respectively. According to IEC 61508 it has to be distinguished between random (stochastic) *hardware* failures and *systematic* failures. Random hardware failures can be quantified, i.e. it is possible to specify a failure rate per hour or day. However, systematic failures cannot be quantified exactly. In other words, failures that can be quantified are random hardware failures, the remainder of failures are systematic failures. Systematic failures endanger the systematic safety integrity whilst hardware failures jeopardize the hardware safety integrity. Both together comprise the *safety integrity*: the probability that a safety related system executes the required safety functions under all defined circumstances within a fixed period of time [IEC61-4].

Efficiency of measures like online self tests to ensure hardware integrity is categorized by the diagnostic coverage. A higher diagnostic coverage means more faults related to a hardware component must be detected that do not result in a dangerous failure. Measures with a low diagnostic coverage must detect stuck-at faults: a fault category, which shows a constant "0" or "1" on the pins of the component. Others with a high diagnostic coverage must detect faults of the DC-fault model (DC = direct current). It incorporates stuck-at fault, line break, high impedance outputs and short circuit between signal lines [IEC61-2]. On the contrary, performance of measures to ensure systematic integrity is categorized by 3 levels: 'low', 'medium' and 'high', depending on the target safety integrity level.

With the aforementioned in mind, a target SIL can be reached by a low hardware fault tolerance and using high efficient measures, i.e. with a high diagnostic coverage, to ensure a high level of hardware integrity and a low probability of undetected dangerous failures. On the other hand, a target SIL is achieved by integrating measures with a low diagnostic coverage and therefore a low SFF, i.e. a rather high probability of undetected dangerous failures, but a hardware tolerance of one or two. In other words, the hardware architecture is a function of the target SIL and the SFF (Table 4-2).

Table 4-2. Safety integrity of deployed hardware (IEC 61508)

Safe failure fraction	Hardware fault tolerance[1]		
	0	1	2
< 60%	not possible	SIL 1	SIL 2
60% - < 90%	SIL 1	SIL 2	SIL 3
90% - < 99%	SIL 2	SIL 3	SIL 4
≥ 99%	SIL 3	SIL 4	SIL 4

[1]) A hardware fault tolerance of N denotes that N+1 faults cause a loss of the safety status of the system.

Beside hardware integrity also systematic integrity has to be granted. Part of the systematic integrity is software integrity. It is ensured by first of all specifying a software safety lifecycle model based on the V-model [BRO93]. Second, non-functional and functional measures are specified for the various lifecycle stages. For example, the use of design tools during specification or use of performance tests during integration of the software onto the target hardware.

In conclusion, all the safety topics mentioned are spread over the seven parts of the standard. They were published by the International Electrotechnical Commission (IEC) between 1998 and 2000. In 2001 it also became a European standard (EN). Part 1 is dedicated to the safety lifecycle model, part 2 to hardware related topics to be considered, part 3 to software related issues. Part 4 conveys information on the definition of terms used in the standard. Part 5 gives examples of how to reach target safety integrity levels and part 6 provides guidelines of how to apply part 2 and part 3 of the standard. In the end, part 7 lists functional and non-functional safety measures used to reach a target safety integrity level.

4.2 Security and the Common Criteria

The standard IEC 15408 [IEC15] – for historical purpose called Common Criteria (CC) – is a basis of evaluation of security properties of IT products and systems. CC specify a set of requirements for the security functions of IT products and systems. Additionally, it gives requirements for assurance measures applied to the security functions during security evaluation. As a consequence, CC permits to compare results of independent security evaluations.

The goal of the Common Criteria are to develop a full lifecycle consensus based security engineering standard [HER03, p. 10]. It does not cover for example operational security such as mentioned in [WOO07]. Operational security is discussed in ISO 17799 [ISO17]. Moreover, it does not address physical or personnel security, or administrative security measures.

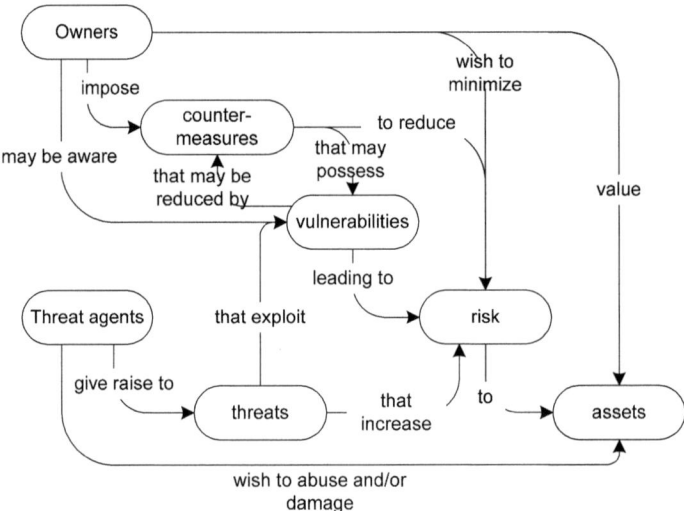

Fig. 4-1 Security concept [IEC15-1]

The Common Criteria include two basic concepts: a *security concept* and an *evaluation concept*. The idea of the first one (Fig. 4-1) is that owners of assets analyze the possible threats to the assets. They determine which threats apply to their environment. These threats result in risk to the assets. To reduce the risk to assets, countermeasures are required that themselves may posses vulnerabilities and lead to a risk to the assets.

The evaluation concept is based on the idea that evaluation, i.e. active investigation of the IT product or system that is to be trusted, gives evidence of assurance and assurance techniques produce assurance. Owners of assets require assurance because it gives confidence that countermeasures minimize risk to their assets. The standard presents a framework in which an effective evaluation is possible by defining a way to derive requirements and a specification. It, however, does not mandate any specific lifecycle model.

The security concept is based on a catalogue of security *functional requirements* [IEC15-2] that describe the security behavior of a Target of Evaluation (TOE). On the other hand, the security evaluation concept is implemented by a catalogue of security *assurance requirements* [IEC15-3] that define the scope, depth and rigor of evaluation of a TOE, i.e. IT product or system that is subject of evaluation. Both, security and assurance requirements catalogues, are categorized in classes. Security requirements of a class share a common focus. The name of an assurance class indicates the covered topics. Each class consists of different families of security requirements which share same security objectives. Families are finally divided into components that are the smallest set of requirements (Fig. 4-2).

Security requirements from the different functional security classes (Table 4-3) are chosen depending on the security objectives. Security assurance requirements are selected from various assurance classes (Table 4-3). Evaluation assurance requirements intend to rise the quality of the product by demanding design, organizational and analytic measures.

In the classes, there are principal security requirements and supporting requirements. The latter are dependent on the ones mentioned first. In addition, it is foreseen to state security functional and corresponding evaluation assurance requirements explicitly in case of issues not covered in the Common Criteria. Put another way, security requirement specification or security design need not to be limited to the security requirements catalogues.

International Standards

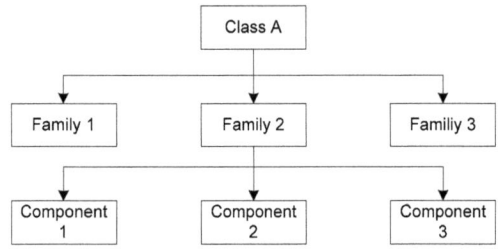

Fig. 4-2 Hierarchical structure of security functional and security assurance requirements

Within the Common Criteria a security requirement specification is referred to as protection profile. It is a formal document that expresses an implementation independent set of security functional and security assurance requirements for an IT product that meets specific consumer needs [IEC15-1]. By contrast, a security target, i.e. a security design, is an implementation dependent response to a protection profile that is used a basis to develop of Target of Evaluation (TOE). The security target includes security functions and the strength of functions (SOF), and measures. A physical implementation of a security target is called a TOE. A single protection profile can be instantiated by multiple security targets (one to many), whereas a TOE is always derived from just one security target (one to one).

Evaluation of a protection profile and security target, respectively, is performed by means of assurance requirements stated in the class 'Protection profile evaluation' and 'Security Target Evaluation'. The other assurance classes listed in Table 4-3 are used to evaluate a TOE in its different lifecycle stages. In contrast to the class of a protection profile or security target, such evaluation assurance requirements are depending on the chosen level of evaluation assurance (EAL). A higher EAL reduces the likelihood of vulnerabilities and increase the amount of confidence, but the effort is getting greater because a larger portion of the system is included in the evaluation process In addition, more details of the design are covered and the evaluation process is carried out in a more structured and formal manner the higher the EAL is required.

The Common Criteria specify seven evaluation assurance levels (EAL) for TOE evaluation. Each EAL consists of a set of requirements from the different assurance classes referred to as package. The EAL is chosen regarding the intended use of the TOE. E.g., EAL 1 is appropriate for such environments where no serious security threats are anticipated [HER03, p. 180]. Or, EAL 3 is called methodically tested and checked, and provides a moderate level of confidence [IEC15-3]. It includes at least one component from every assurance class. EAL packages can be augmented with additional assurance requirements from all classes and then called e.g. EAL 3 augmented. However, it is strictly forbidden to remove any requirement from an EAL package.

Table 4-3 Security functional classes [IEC15-2] and security assurance classes [IEC15-3]

Security functional classes	Security assurance classes
Communications	Configuration management
Cryptographic support	Delivery and operation
Identification and authentication	Development
Privacy	Guidance documents
Protection of the trusted security functions	Lifecycle support
Resource utilization	Protection profile evaluation
Security audit	Security Target evaluation
Security management	Vulnerability assessment
TOE access	Tests
Trusted path/channels	
User data protection	

All aforementioned topics are covered in the standard IEC 15408 in three parts: part 1 – introduction and the general model, part 2 – security functional requirements and part 3 – security assurance requirements. The second edition of the standard, published by the International Organization for Standardization (ISO) and the International Electrotechnical Commission (IEC) in 2005 is based on the Common Criteria Version 2.3.

In 1993 the Common Criteria (CC) project was started to harmonize US, Canadian and European security criteria and create a single set of IT security criteria. After some draft versions were published and extensive reviews were made, CC version 2.1 was finally standardized as ISO/IEC 15408 in 1999. The CC are considered *the* international standard for information technology security [HER03, p. 1]: a reason why CC are applied in the common approach.

5. Survey on Safety and Security Approaches

The two objectives of the common approach are first to find a way of integrating safety and security, and second to specify a 'development-use' model. Integration is accomplished by harmonizing safety and security, and not unifying both domains. Different ways of safety and security harmonization are presented in the first subchapter. It must be noted that some ways are called 'unified' by their authors, although they mean integrating safety and security without inventing new methodologies.

Issues relating to the lifecycle of a system are discussed in the second subchapter. Because of no complete lifecycle approaches being publicly available that deals with safety and security, lifecycle issues in the field of safety and security are outlined. In addition, since a requirement on the common approach is to be widely accepted by safety, security and BACS people, lifecycle model related terminology is in adherence with the international standard IEC 12207 [IEC12].

5.1 Harmonizing Safety and Security

In accordance with [EAM99], within the thesis harmonizing means to integrate safety and security by using standard concepts and methodologies from both disciplines. The intention is not to reinvent what is state of the art as stated in [SCH05], but to design the common approach in a way so that is likely accepted by safety, security and building automation and control (BACS) people, and therefore adheres to international standards.

An approach to integrate safety and security is presented in [EAM99]. Integration is performed at requirements level. As the safety risk analysis process and the security risk analysis process show quite a lot similarities, it is argued that safety and security can be integrated; moreover, because both deal with risks and both safety and security risk analysis result in constraints. Additionally, safety and security use protective measures and produce requirements to be considered of great importance.

The approach discussed in [EAM99] suggests developing safety and security requirements absolutely independent from each other in parallel. Safety requirements are determined by defining the system boundaries and functions first. Next, preliminary hazard identification is carried out in order to record hazards and hazardous failures. Third, a preliminary hazard analysis is performed to identify the functional failures that could result to hazardous states. Finally, the safety requirements are specified due to the inputs from the aforementioned activities and other sources such as good engineering practice.

Security requirement specification is set up by first defining the system: identify security relevant information, data to be handled and the system configuration, and account the role of the system. Second, security threats are assessed applying a process specified in the Orange Book [TCS85], but also influenced by the European ITSEC standard [ITS91]. Threat sources are identified and evaluated to determine the level of assurance required to protect the system. In the end, security measures are defined. Such measures necessary to achieve the defined level of security are described.

The safety requirements and security requirements were specified. Now the interaction between safety and security is investigated. Two types of interaction are mentioned: requirements can be conflicting and/or inconsistent, or inter-related. Conflicting means that the requirements are incompatible. The best example is a door. In case of a defect, fail safe would mean the door is open, fail secure the door is closed. The other form of interaction covers the possibility that a security requirement is specified because of safety analysis or vice versa. Such requirements are called derived requirements. The two forms of interactions are distinguished because of executing the conflict resolution properly. A change of a derived requirement influences the other domain and might cause new problems, whilst resolving a conflict between conflicting requirements has no impact on the corresponding domain.

Whereas [EAM99] discusses the integration of safety and security on requirements level, [STO06] focuses on the risk framework and presents a unified safety/security risk framework. With respect to the definition of 'unified' in the thesis, it is an approach to harmonize the risk frameworks. A standard safety risk framework and a standard security risk framework are used and an interface between both frameworks is design. In other words, output of the security framework is seen as input to the safety framework.

In detail, the security framework defines vulnerability and threat source as *the potential of harmful security events*. Such events result in threats. The impact and likelihood of occurrence of the threat finally leads to a level of risk. The safety framework defines undesired events as *hazards*. The occurrence of a specific hazardous event with likelihood and resulting impact leads to a mishap. Impact multiplied with likelihood of occurrence of a mishap causes a level of risk. Harmonizing the both frameworks is performed by considering the potential of harmful security events to be a safety hazard.

In [SCH05] a unified approach of safety and security for designing complex embedded systems is proposed. 'Unified' again means harmonization of safety and security. The approach is suggested since it is stated that security impacts have severe safety impact and vice versa.

The international standard IEC 61508 [IEC61] is taken as source for safety and the lifecycle model in the standard is the model where to integrate safety and security. It is mentioned that safety and security follow the same steps at requirements level: security analysis and risk/hazard analysis, security requirements and safety requirements, security design and safety design. Security related topics are taken from the international standard ISO 17799 [ISO17] in order to avoid specifying a new methodology and terminology.

5.2 Lifecycle Approaches

The 'development-use' model is realized by a lifecycle model as mentioned in subchapter 2.2. Such a model specifies a structured way of developing and using a BACS. It covers all phases in the life of a system starting with the concept phase and ending with the decommissioning of the system. As a result, systematic failures and vulnerabilities can be reduced and the level of quality with regard to safety and security is increased.

In the following, terms related to lifecycles are introduced first. They are being used as terms in the common approach to describe the safety-security lifecycle. Second, starting with subchapter 5.2.2, some realizations of lifecycles in the safety and security domain are presented.

5.2.1 Terminology

A lifecycle model specifies requirements for the different phases in the life of a system. On the contrary to system requirements that specify *what* to do to receive the desired system, lifecycle requirements specify *how* to proceed during the lifecycle phases of the system. As shown in Fig. 5-1, system requirements are categorized in subsystem requirements and further grouped into hardware and software ones. Such a categorization is not only valid for requirements, but also for lifecycles: a system lifecycle covering the life of the system; a subsystem or entity lifecycle specifying requirements on the development and use of a subsystem such as a node; a hardware and software lifecycle dealing with issues related to hard- and software.

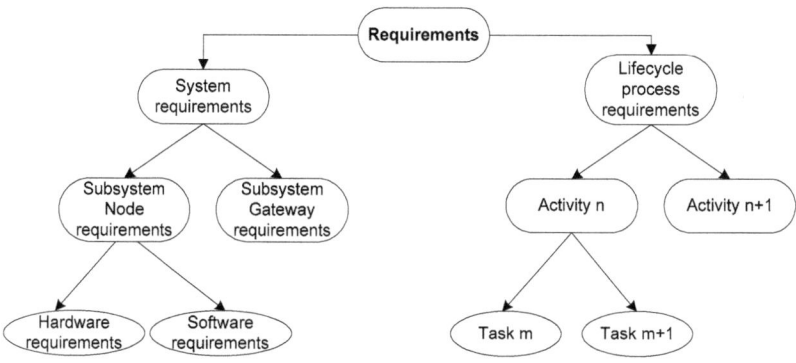

Fig. 5-1 Types of requirements

Lifecycle requirements are referred to as tasks in [IEC12]. Tasks are grouped into various activities and activities are summarized in a process (Fig. 5-1). According to [IEC12] a lifecycle process is "a set of interrelated activities, which transform inputs into outputs". For instance, the activity is called 'Establish security objectives'. It receives as input assumptions, threats and the organizational security policy. Task 1 is 'Define security objectives.', task 2 is 'Categorize them into detective, preventive and corrective objectives.'. The output is a list of security objectives being input to the subsequent activity.

[IEC12] specifies three different types of processes: five primary, eight supporting and four organizational lifecycle processes. Primary lifecycle processes specify activities and tasks of the primary parties during the lifecycle. The primary parties are the acquirer (acquisition process), the supplier (supply process), the developer (development process), the operator (operation process), and the maintainer (maintenance process).

Supporting lifecycle processes (Table 5-1) support another process in order to increase the change of succeeding and to raise the quality. Supporting processes are called by another process. For example, development process executes supporting documentation process to record the information on system requirements. The output of the documentation process is a system requirements specification. Or, at the end of development validation process is called to check if the system satisfies its intended use.

Table 5-1 Supporting lifecycle processes [IEC12]

Supporting lifecycle process	Activity
1. Documentation	Recording information produced by a lifecycle process; e.g., plans, specifications
2. Configuration management	Configuration identification, control, evaluation, release management; e.g., identification of software artifacts
3. Quality assurance	Product assurance and process assurance; e.g., define procedures for review process
4. Verification	Verify process, requirements, documents; e.g., check project planning requirements
5. Validation	Validate requirements; e.g., ensure that the system satisfies its intended use
6. Joint review	Review project management, technical issues; e.g., check whether specifications are complete
7. Audit	Determining compliance with requirements or plans; e.g., test data complies with specification
8. Problem resolution	Analyze and resolve problems; e.g., provide a report describing the problems

The third type of processes is the four organizational lifecycle processes: management, infrastructure, improvement and training. The processes are set up by an organization and not specific to projects or systems. They are an underlying structure for primary and supporting lifecycle processes.

The management process specifies the basic activities of the management necessary to execute other lifecycle processes (see Fig. 4-2). The infrastructure process provides the activities for establishing the underlying structure of a lifecycle process. Activities related to controlling, improving, measuring lifecycle process are subsumed in the improvement process. In the end, the training process comprises activities for providing trained personnel.

5.2.2 Generic Model

The IEEE standard 1074-2006 [IEE17] provides a process for creating a (software) lifecycle process. I.e., it defines requirements for building a lifecycle process adapted to the needs of a specific project. Consequently, it defines a pool of activities that are mapped to the lifecycle model and that create a lifecycle process together with organizational activities like the ones outlined in subchapter 5.2.1.

Activities are grouped into project management, pre-development, development, post-development and supporting activities. Each activity consists of three parts: *input* information – the source to be transformed –, *description* – actions to be performed to accomplish transformation – and *output* information – result of transformation. In addition, an entry and exit criteria for every activity is defined. To start an activity, at least one element of the required input information must be present. To exit an activity, all output information has to be generated.

Lifecycle models not necessarily intend to mandate a sequential procedure, where activity n has to be finished before starting with activity $n+1$. [IEE17] foresees three ways of mapping an activity to a lifecycle model. First, an activity is mapped as an instance, i.e. it is mapped once. It takes all specified inputs, processes it and delivers the complete output. A chain of instances of activities in a lifecycle model results in a sequential procedure. Second, an entity is mapped as iteration. Some of the input is available and hence some of the output is produced. The activity is repeated as long as the complete output has not been created. Third, supporting activities such as verification activities are invoked by other activities directly relating to a lifecycle phase. Such activities exist in parallel to others, perform a specific function and then return to the invoking activity. For example, the activity 'Define and develop software requirements.' invokes the activity 'documentation' to receive a record of the software requirements, i.e. a software requirements specification. The invoking activity is considered to be finished, only if the invoked activity (e.g., documentation) was processed successfully.

5.2.3 Safety

As already mentioned in subchapter 2.2, in the area of safety systems are often developed according to a lifecycle because it is a structured way of developing and hence reduces the number of systematic failure and raises safety integrity, respectively.

In [HAM91] a holistic safety lifecycle for software engineering is presented that is based on the V-Model [BRO93]. It is extended in a way so that it starts with the hazard analysis and risk assessment. Results of both activities are input the first step of the V-Model: requirement specification. The final step in the lifecycle approach is safety validation where the result of development is checked against the safety requirements specification.

The disadvantage of the aforementioned approach is that a concept phase and the whole use phase, i.e. commissioning or modification is not covered. The lifecycle approach mentioned in [BAT96] includes a concept and scope definition as well as topics related installation and modification. That is important because a wrong concept may lead to design faults and to a development of the 'wrong' system. A waste of time and effort, and increasing costs are the consequence.

A lot of ideas discussed in [HAM91], [BAT96] and of course many other publications are included into the safety lifecycle standardized in IEC 61508 [IEC61-1], mentioned already in subchapter 4.1. The safety lifecycle covers all stages in the life of a safety related system starting from the concept phase and ending with decommissioning. It consists of sixteen stages that guide through the development and use of hardware and software safety related systems.

This lifecycle consists of a hardware and software realization stage that includes further activities referring to the hardware and software: another lifecycle to realize the hardware [IEC61-2] and the software [IEC61-3]. Realization of software should be in accordance with the V-Model.

5.2.4 Security

Due to the increasing connectivity of computers, the extensibility (extension of functionality by means of updates) and the growth of complexity of systems, the security problem has been growing. Especially, software is riddled with software defects: bugs such as buffer overflow or design flaws like inconsistent error handling [MCG06, p. 17]. For that reason Microsoft started with the 'Trustworthy Computing Initiative' in 2002 [LIP04].

As outlined in [LIP04], the trustworthy computing initiative specifies security related activities for the different lifecycle phases. Activities can be grouped into a security process (a supporting lifecycle process as shown in Fig. 5-2) that is supporting the primary processes: requirements, design, implementation, verification, release, support and servicing. In addition, an organizational lifecycle process, training, is addressed by the initiative.

The security process comprises seven activities that in turn include some tasks. Activity during requirement process is called *inception*. A typical task is 'Identify security requirements'. *Design and threat modeling* is performed in the design process. Assets and threats to the assets are identified as well as the risk resulting from the threats is assessed. Moreover, the security architecture is documented. *Guidelines and best practice* activity is carried out during implementation. Tasks are the development of test plans or adherence to coding standards and the use of tools. The verification process includes the security activity *security push*. On the one hand the reviews of the threat model and code are performed and attack testing is executed. The *final security review* yet again reviews the threat model and the new and unfixed bugs, and completes penetration testing. Finally, the activity *security response feedback* and its tasks such as 'Processes evaluated' are executed during support and service process.

In [AME05] a survey on security in the system development lifecycle is provided. A summary of security related activities in the different lifecycle phases is given. However, there are not mentioned any specific lifecycle model and measures to ensure security, nor is security seen as a supporting process. The intention is to introduce a general approach to security architecture: security activities are highlighted, but implementation of activities is not addressed.

The lifecycle of a system is separated into seven phases. The lifecycle starts with the investigation *phase* that includes the investigation of the project scope, the evaluation of existing resources, and the definition of security goals and the security policy. The *analysis phase* is the second phase and concerned with identifying the threats to assets and with classifying the risk resulting from the threat. Next, in the *logical design phase* it is necessary to select the applications to be used, and the data and structure support. The result of the phase is a so called security blueprint as well as a plan is developed including a way of how to response to incidents. Solutions developed in the previous phase are realized in the *physical design phase*. Appropriate system security, network security, database security and software security mechanism are defined. In the *implementation phase* mechanism specified before are implemented on the target system. After that, the system is verified and validated. Moreover, since not everyone is a security expert, it is recommended to have an independent third party that evaluates the system. Such evaluation process can be performed according to the requirements in Common Criteria [IEC15-3]. Finally, *maintenance and change phase* deals with monitoring the secure system to become aware of attacks. And a security management model is required to manage and plan security during operation.

Whereas the previous approach mentioned in [AME05] is highlighting the basic security activities in the different lifecycle phases, [MCG06] presents an approach for putting software security into practice. Proactive design and exploit driven testing built on a foundation of risk management are the key factors of the approach. It is based on three pillars: applied risk management, seven so called touchpoints or software security best practices, and knowledge. The approach presented in [MCG06] does not specify a security lifecycle model. Applying the three pillars to a standard lifecycle model, however, results in a security lifecycle.

Risk management is introduced as an activity to be carried out throughout the whole lifecycle. The idea is to identify, assess, track and understand security risk during the different phases of the lifecycle. That philosophy is implemented in the risk management framework (RMF).

The seven touchpoints are software security best practices and are applied to various software artifacts. It is stressed that they are executed in an iterative way. As mentioned before, no specific lifecycle model is defined. However, it is assumed that every software development process produces similar artifacts.

Finally, the third pillar is called knowledge. The term summarizes the gathering, encapsulating and sharing of security knowledge used as a foundation for software security practices. That is, a knowledge management is required that should help to evolve a software security culture in a company. Knowledge gained must be circulated to other people by means of training activities and is used as input to the various touchpoints.

5.3 Conclusion

The common approach faces two challenges: first to find a way of integrating safety and security, and second to specify a 'development-use' model. In the context of the thesis integration means harmonizing safety and security, i.e. using standard concepts and methodologies from both disciplines.

Safety and security can be harmonized on different levels: requirement level [EAM99], risk level [STO06] or during the whole lifecycle [SCH05]. In the thesis safety and security are harmonized throughout the whole lifecycle since safety and security related issues are present in every lifecycle stage. E.g., safety and security is relevant in the requirements specification, but also in the installation stage. It must be ensured that security keys are distributed securely and configuration data is stored on every node with a very high probability.

Mentioned many times, the 'development-use' model is based on a lifecycle model as it is common practice in the safety domain (see subchapter 5.2.3). A lifecycle model is chosen because it is a structured way of developing and using a safe-secure system. Hence, it reduces the number of systematic failures resulting for instance from a design fault. In addition, it eases traceability of the work performed since a set of clearly specified requirements is available. The fact also makes verification and validation easier [HAM91].

Safety and security requirements given during the different stages in the lifecycle model are organized as stated in IEC 12207 [IEC12] and shown in Fig. 5-2. Supporting lifecycle processes such as documentation or verification include activities to ensure a defined level of safety and security. Additionally, four organizational lifecycle processes are employed to provide an underlying structure. Both set of processes are equal to the ones specified in [IEC12] because such activities are also included in IEC 61508 and the Common Criteria. For instance in IEC 61508 activities of the organizational lifecycle processes are subsumed by the term functional safety management. Or, in [MCG06, pp. 259] when discussing security best practice activities it is the third pillar: knowledge.

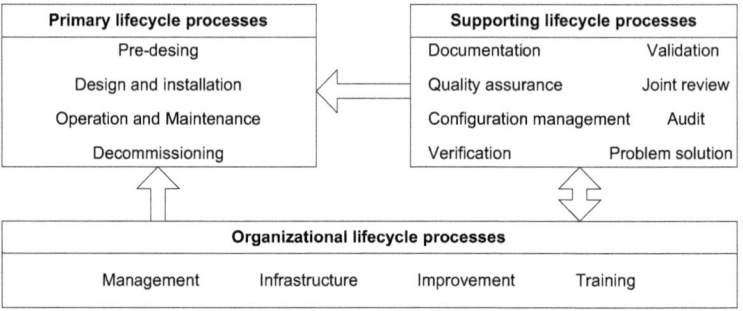

Fig. 5-2 Safety-security lifecycle processes

In contrast to [IEC12] there are only four primary lifecycle processes since the common approach does not cover topics related to project acquisition or supply. The focus of attention is on the four primary processes within the thesis and they are outlined in chapter 6 when presenting the safety-security lifecycle model, i.e. the flow of activities in the different primary processes proposed by the author.

According to the methodology presented in [IEE17] supporting lifecycle processes are either instantiated, i.e. each activity is finished before the next one starts or implemented as iteration. Primary lifecycle processes and their activities in the safety-security lifecycle model (Fig. 6-1) are run through more than once to allow for delivering first prototypes in a project soon. That is, the lifecycle model in chapter 6 does not mandate a sequential flow of activities.

6. Common Approach

The common approach to functional safety and system security in building automation and control systems (BACS), proposed by the author and presented in the following, is based on a lifecycle model. Generally, it is a model of the life of a system, including all the activities needed to specify, develop, operate, maintain and dispose of a system. The basic idea of the safety-security lifecycle presented in Fig. 6-1 is to use the safety lifecycle from IEC 61508 and integrate the security approach specified in Common Criteria (CC) [IEC15]. Requirements how to proceed are given for every stage of the system life. Moreover, activities are added by the author to consider safety and security dependences resulting from harmonizing safety and security.

The common approach specifies a procedure that allows for certification of the safe and secure system by (national) evaluation and certification authorities such as TUV in Germany [TUD08]. Since there are only authorities that certify a product with regard to safety *or* security, a way is presented how to integrate safety requirements into the CC security model and how to incorporate security requirements into the IEC 61508 safety concept. Even though, the structure of safe and secure documents (e.g., protection profile and safety requirements specification) differs, the security certification "approach is similar to that followed to verify safety-critical embedded software systems (see IEC 61508)" [HER03, p. 177].

The lifecycle in Fig. 6-1 is separated into 4 primary processes. Each of them invokes supporting processes and is based on organizational processes (Fig. 5-2). Noteworthy to say, stages not including the word *overall* (i.e. system wide) must be performed for every subsystem such as a node or gateway (entity lifecycle):

1. Pre-design process – stage 1 to 11
2. Design and installation process – stage 12 to 17

3. Operation and maintenance process – stage 18 and 19
4. Decommissioning process – stage 20

6.1 Pre-design

The pre-design of a safe-secure BACS is the first process of the safety-security lifecycle model. Stages 1 to 4 are following IEC 61508 (refer to subchapter 4.1), stages 5 to 8 are following the Common Criteria (see subchapter 4.2). Stages 9 is an additional activities included by the author to handle dependencies between safety and security. Stages 10 and 11 already consider safety and security issues.

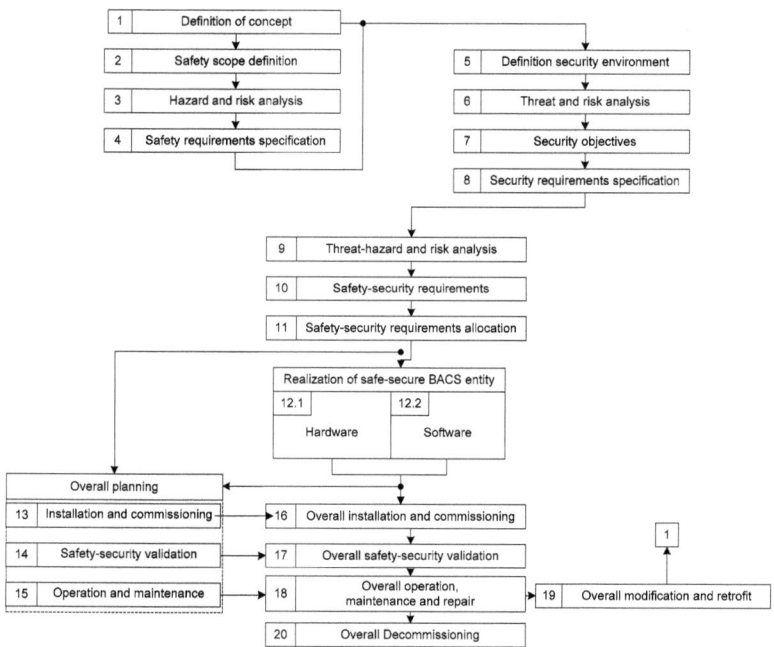

Fig. 6-1 Safety-security lifecycle model

The pre-design process begins with the *definition of the concept* that is input to the safety dependent and the security dependent part. First of all the purpose and the scope of the BACS in general and its entities in particular must be defined. It is important to know what the BACS is used for, its field of application: either to cool server rooms in a huge administration building or to heat and cool two operation rooms in a hospital. Moreover, it is required to specify the scope: Are there 10000 or only 100 nodes in the BACS? Are they connected to an intranet or even to the Internet via gateways? Next, the physical environment has to be investigated. It includes checking the environment of the nodes and the gateways regarding EMC interference, temperature, interaction with other systems and so on, but also people affected by and working with the BACS. In addition, possible sources of hazardous events have to be identified, especially with regard to the environment of the BACS. Such events can result for example from aging of the hardware, human failures or stochastic failures. Finally, social, economical, legal questions are taken into consideration – only mentioned shortly at this point, but these topics are also of great importance.

The next activity is called the *safety scope definition*. It specifies the scope of the BACS required to be investigated in a hazard and risk analysis. Put another way, the boundaries of the BACS and its entities are defined that are analyzed regarding hazardous events and their associated risk.

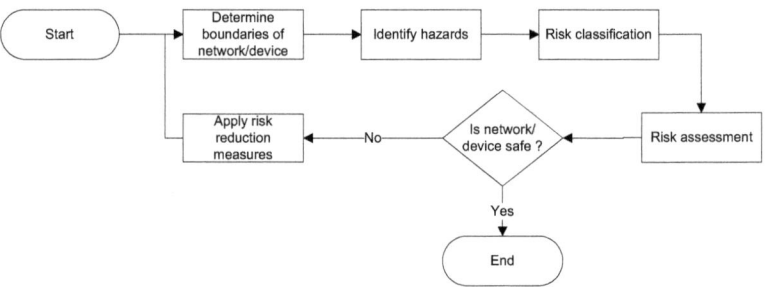

Fig. 6-2 Iterative procedure to achieve required level of safety

The *hazard and risk analysis* aims at identifying typical hazards in BACS. Hazards resulting from failures on the network as well as the ones coming from nodes and gateways, respectively, must be considered. Additionally, the reasons for the hazards are described and the risk associated with the hazards is determined, i.e. a risk assessment is performed. Carrying out a hazard and risk analysis is always an iterative procedure as shown in Fig. 6-2 [WRA07, p. 4]. Whereas most of the statements in Fig. 6-2 are self-explaining, the statement "Is network/device safe?" has to be discussed in detail. A device is safe if the risk is below a tolerable risk level. In other words, the residual failure probability of a failure per hour causing a hazard is lower a defined target level. As mentioned in subchapter 4.1., IEC 61508 specifies such levels, called safety integrity levels (SIL). In short, a device or network is safe if the target SIL is reached.

The hazard analysis can be performed in two ways [BOE07, pp. 80]:

1. Bottom-up search: The chronological method of failure propagation is followed. The original source of the incident is examined and after that step by step the facilities affected by the failure are investigated. The Failure Mode and Effects Analysis (FMEA) [WIT95] is an example of a bottom-up approach.

2. Top-down search: The hazard is taken as starting point and the reason for this hazard is examined to finally detect the source of the hazard. Take the Fault Tree Analysis (FTA) [WIT95] as an example.

The result of the hazard analysis is a list of hazardous events coming from the network and the devices. Typical hazardous events on the network are loss, insertion, corruption of a message due to crosstalk or delay of a message because of congestion on the network. Hazardous events on a device refer to random hardware failures resulting from faults in the I/O component or volatile memory as well as systematic failures in the software, for instance the operating system.

Following the identification of hazards, a level of risk of the hazardous event going to happen is specified. After that the risk is assessed. Generally, risk assessment is possible by means of a quantitative or qualitative approach. The quantitative one uses numbers and mathematical rules (calculus of probabilities) to calculate the risk. As a consequence, it is necessary to specify a maximum tolerable risk target, e.g. the maximum tolerable risk of fatality to an employee or of an accident at home. [TOR92] and [RRP01] are giving a lot of information on that topic. The risk of random hardware failures e.g., on a node can also be quantified by failure rates of the hardware components. In literature such as [GIE95] or [LIG02] failure rates for standard hardware components are listed.

The IEC 61508 standard also allows for a qualitative approach to assess risk. A well known mechanism is the risk graph as shown in Fig. 6-3. In IEC 61508 four parameters are specified as input and the output is a corresponding SIL.

1. C – extent of hazard (severity): 4 different levels C_1 (insignificant) to C_4 (disastrous).

2. F – frequency of occurrence: 4 different levels F_1 (rare) to F_4 (very often).

3. P – possibility of avoidance: 2 different levels P_1 (possible) and P_2 (not possible).

4. W – probability of occurrence: 3 different levels W_1 (not likely) to W_3 (very likely).

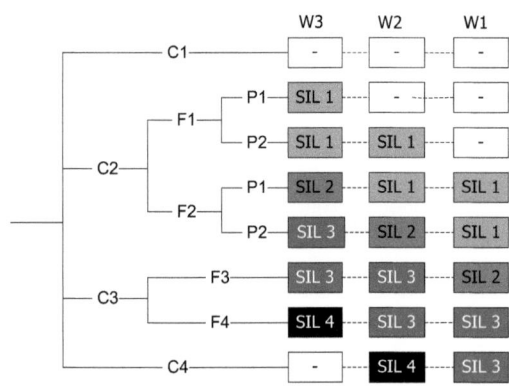

Fig. 6-3 Risk graph [IEC61]

After hazard identification and risk assessment it is either necessary to apply additional risk reduction measures or the target SIL has been reached (Fig. 6-2). Risk reduction can only be achieved by performing safety functions derived from safety requirements, both specified in the *safety requirements specification*. It is distinguished between safety functions requirements and safety integrity requirements. The first one specifies requirements on functions whereas the latter requirements on the integrity of a function. Safety integrity requirements can also be seen as performance requirements [IEC61-0].

- A safety function requirement is 'Detect a failure (wrong values stored) in the volatile memory of a node to ensure hardware integrity.' A corresponding safety integrity requirement is 'The diagnostic coverage[1] has to be 90%.'

---

[1] See subchapter 4.1 for explanation of diagnostic coverage.

- Another safety function requirement is 'Detect systematic faults in the hardware or software design'. The safety integrity requirement is 'Because of target SIL 3, efficiency must be of level 'medium' as stated in IEC 61508.'

Safety functions are derived from the safety functions requirements. It is not necessarily required that one requirement maps to one safety function. A safety function requirements can map to various functions whereas different functions may map to a single requirement. Safety functions, in turn, are implemented by different safety measures. The kind of measure is determined by the safety integrity requirement.

- A safety function derived from the first requirement is 'Use of memory test on start-up and during operation'. A safety measure is 'Implementation of memory test 'walk-path'. Its diagnostic coverage is high (90%) and therefore the safety integrity requirement is met.

- A requirement on the detection of systematic failure in the hardware and software design results in the safety function 'Monitor the program flow of the safety related software on a node'. The safety integrity should be of level 'medium'. As a result, the safety measure is 'Monitor program flow by using key techniques'. Such techniques are described in [HOE86, pp. 7-86].

In short, safety requirements specification includes a specification of the functions and integrity requirements. Additionally, requirements on the safety functions and the safety measures implementing safety functions are defined. Finally, safety requirements also affect the hardware architecture. As shown in Fig. 4-2, a target SIL can be reached by either increasing the fault tolerance or the safe failure fraction (SFF). In case of SIL 3 three ways are possible: a very high SFF, i.e. detecting more than 99% of all dangerous failures with highly efficient measures, and a fault tolerance of zero, i.e. just a single safety channel; or a SFF between 90%-99% and a hardware fault tolerance of one (two channels); or a SFF in the range of 60%-90% and a hardware fault tolerance of two (three channels).

All that information is also used as input to the security dependent part of the safety and security lifecycle (Fig. 6-1). It starts with the *definition of security environment*. It comprises the physical environment as well as the list of assets requiring protection, already including the safety requirements. The physical environment has already been investigated in stage 1 of the lifecycle. However, hardware architecture of entities (nodes, gateway) may have changed due to safety requirements.

Consequently, it has to be reexamined in detail. For example, it is 'good practice' to use redundancy to ensure a target level, in BACS for instance accomplished by a 1oo2 (speak: one out of two) hardware architecture [NOV07]. Such an architecture consists of two independent channels that execute a given job, but must agree on the result unanimously. Put another way, the hardware of a node is duplicated (e.g., two microcontrollers) and every microcontroller performs the safety functions. The output of the function is only valid, if the safety function on both microcontroller results in the same answer.

Second, definition of security environment includes identification and valuation of assets, i.e. information or resources requiring protection as well as a statement of assumptions. In [HER03, pp. 68] three categories of assets are identified:

1. TOE (Target of Evaluation: node, gateway) operational data that the TOE stores, processes or transports; for example, data from sensors, processed results of measurements on node side, traffic data sent among nodes or gateway.

2. TOE hardware, software and firmware on node and gateway side (IT environment): Assets are node resources such as the safety related software, cryptographic keys, the security software itself, the (redundant) hardware. Other assets are the hardware and software of the gateway.

3. Operational data and documentation used to operate and maintain the TOE. Such assets are security incident lists, security configuration and management information. These types of assets are not investigated within the thesis regarding safeguarding them since it is not BACS specific and therefore standard measures can be applied.

Assets not only must be identified, but also the value of the asset has to be fixed. The value can be determined either by introducing different discrete levels ('high' or 'low') or expressing the value of an asset in terms of money. The first approach is a qualitative, the second a quantitative one.

A description of assumptions conveys information on the security aspects of the environment which the TOE will be used in, i.e. information about the intended usage and the environment of the TOE. An assumption can be: 'All hardware and software of a node critical to security functions are protected from unauthorized modification by hostile insiders or outsiders'.

Next a *threat and risk analysis* is performed. As already shown in Fig. 4-1, threats are resulting from threat agents, i.e. attackers. There are threats directly increasing the risk to assets or exploiting vulnerabilities and indirectly leading to risk. Risk analysis assigns a risk potential to the identified threats, i.e. it values the risk. Finally, a risk assessment is performed where the value of assets is associated with the risk potential of a threat.

In [HER03, p. 74] two categories of potential threats are identified at a high level:

1. Information confidentiality, integrity and availability are compromised accidentally or malicious intentionally by either insiders or outsiders. Those are threats directly increasing risk of an asset. For instance, an unauthorized user performs actions the individual is not authorized to perform, e.g. reading data remotely from a node via a network management tool; or insertion of bogus data onto the network.

2. Failures of hardware, software, communication links and so forth allow an accidental or malicious intentional interruption to operations. In other words, vulnerabilities, e.g. improper operation of software on a node due to a implementation bug, exploited by an attacker lead to risk to assets. Other vulnerabilities may result from weaknesses in the hardware and software architecture, respectively.

Furthermore, the direct and indirect threats are valued. It is possible to assign a risk value to every threat individually or to define classes of threats with the same risk value. The latter requires less effort and forces the developer to structure the threats. [GOR00, p. 73] suggests four groups of assets for a fieldbus system in general: node data, node resources, gateway resources, network traffic. Every threat is assigned to a group and every threat in a group has the same risk level. For example, a threat 'unauthorized user performing traffic analysis' is assigned to the group network traffic; or the threat mentioned before 'reading data remotely from a node via a network management tool' is a threat to node data.

In the end, the risk value of a threat and the value of an asset must be associated with each other. That procedure is called risk assessment and is the basis of further discussion with regard to security objectives. As already mentioned above during describing the safety dependent part of the pre-design, risk can be assessed in a quantitative or qualitative way. If assets are valued in terms of money, risk will be quantified. In [MCG06, pp. 39] a quantified approach called risk management framework is presented. It starts with a description of business goals. They include but are not limited to increasing revenue, reducing development costs or generating high return on investment. Risk is assessed by prioritizing the business goals and which goals are threatened immediately. A qualitative approach of risk assessment is to use a risk matrix [BOE07, pp. 85]. In case of 4 groups of assets and four categories of risk levels a risk matrix identifying the actual risk level can be proposed as shown in Table 6-1 for a BACS.

Table 6-1 Risk matrix for risk assessment

		Probability of risk of threat			
		highest	high	medium	low
Value of asset	highest	highest	highest	high	high
	high	highest	high	high	medium
	medium	high	high	medium	medium
	low	high	medium	medium	low

Table 6-1 has to be read in the following way: 4 columns are specified, each with a different degree of a risk level of a threat. The diverse values of assets are written into 4 rows. The actual risk to an asset can be taken from the matrix. Put another way, the risk matrix shows the likelihood of an asset being a target for various threats and the risk mitigation priority.

After that the *security objectives* are defined that counter all identified threats and their risk to the assets. In addition, assumptions taken and if available the organizational security policy are considered. In detail, at that point is has to be fixed what the Target of Evaluation (TOE such as a node) will and will not do in the context of the security environment. That is, the scope of the TOE is specified.

Security objectives are written for the TOE and the IT environment. Additionally, security objectives can be grouped into three categories [IEC54].

1. Preventive objectives are objectives preventing a threat from being carried out or limiting the ways it can be carried out. For example, 'A security function will protect integrity of information when it is stored.' or 'Nodes are connected to a reliable time source to allow proper synchronization.'

2. Detective objectives detect and monitor the occurrence of threats, e.g. 'A security function will detect the loss of system or data (node or network) integrity.' or 'System activity audit records will be reviewed.'
3. Corrective objectives require the TOE to take actions in response to a threat in order to preserve or return to a secure state or limit any damage. For example, 'The node will return to a predefined secure state after a system failure.'

Security objectives result in security requirements and subsequently in security functions. Security measures, in turn, implement security functions. Security requirements and requirements on the functions and measures are included in the *security requirements specification*. In general, a security requirement maps to one or more security objectives, whereas each security objective maps to at least one security requirement. There are three types of security requirements: functional, assurance and for the IT environment as illustrated in Fig. 6-4.

Security functional requirements are specified to implement one or more security objective(s) of a TOE. Such requirements can be taken from the CC requirements catalogue for functional requirements (Table 4-3) or can be stated explicitly. Moreover, a statement of the minimum strength of function (SOF) level for the functional requirement (SOF-basic, SOF-medium, SOF-high) has to be determined. That is, the performance of every functional requirement is qualified if the function is permutational.

On selecting a security functional requirement, three key factors have to be kept in mind in order not to over- or under-protect a TOE and its asset [HER03, p. 89]:

1. Value of the asset being protected: Refer to asset valuation in stage 5 of the safety and security lifecycle.
2. Intended use of the TOE: Is it a node or a gateway?
3. Actual risk level of an asset identified during risk assessment

In the following, an example is given how to receive a security functional requirement derived from a security objective. Mentioned before, a security objective is: 'A security function will protect integrity of information when it is stored' on a node. Assuming that information means user data, i.e. data that does not affect the operation of any security function such as value of a sensor, a requirement from the functional class 'User data protection' (FDP) is chosen. In particular, the family 'Stored data integrity' (SDI) and the corresponding component FDP_SDI.2 'Stored data integrity monitoring and action' is selected. The more severe component 2 is used, since missing data integrity of sensor data in a safety critical environment can result in fatal consequences on actuator side.

Another type of security requirements are security assurance requirements. As outlined in detail in subchapter 4.2, they define the criteria for evaluating among others a TOE and the security assurance responsibilities and activities. To specify security assurance requirements, first a level of confidence required is chosen regarding the value of assets and the perceived risk of compromise, technical feasibility and evaluation cost and time requirements, respectively [IEC15-3, IEC54]. Next an appropriate evaluation assurance level (EAL) is chosen that corresponds with the level of confidence. For instance, low to medium level of confidence is required. Then EAL 3, methodically tested and checked, is a suitable level of assurance.

An EAL defines an assurance package including numerous security assurance requirements. As a further step it has to be clarified, if these requirements are sufficient to guarantee the desired level of confidence. If not, the EAL package can be enhanced with additional requirements (see subchapter 4.2 for details). However, it is not possible to exclude requirements from an EAL package.

Security objectives related to the operational environment lead to security requirements of the IT environment. Mentioned above, a security objective was that proper synchronization among nodes is necessary. The corresponding IT environment requirement is listed in the functional class 'Protection of TOE security function' (FPT), subclass 'time stamps' (STM), component 1: 'The TOE security function shall be able to provide time stamps for its own use'.

Functional and operational (IT environment) requirements result in various security functions, assurance requirements in defined security assurance measures (Fig. 6-4). Security requirements enforce a security policy and are implemented by security measures. In the end, requirements on the different security functions and their mechanisms as well as requirements on the security assurance measures are specified.

To receive a security function, the following procedure is used. A security requirement is 'Stored data integrity monitoring and action', i.e. data on a node must be regularly checked for integrity and in case of corruption action must be taken. The strength of function (SOF) is specified with level 'medium'. A security function is 'integrity check'. A suitable security measure may be 'Use a hash functions and hash the data. Encipher the hash value with a secret key'. Since SOF-medium is required, the secure hash algorithm SHA-1 [LAB95] and a 128 bit key may be applied.

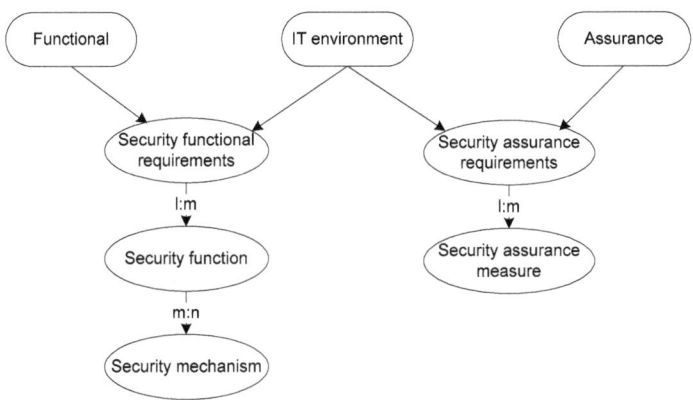

Fig. 6-4 Types of security requirements

Security assurance measures are derived from security assurance requirements. Depending on the chosen evaluation assurance level (EAL), different requirements must be met. Again, each security assurance requirement must map to at least one security assurance measure whereas each assurance measure has to map to at least one requirement (Fig. 6-4). Furthermore, it is necessary to describe how the evidence elements of a safety assurance requirement have been achieved, i.e. what measures have been applied.

For example, EAL 3 includes the requirement ADV_FSP.1 'Informal functional specification' taken from the family 'Functional specification' (FSP) and the class 'Development' (ADV). That requirement can be satisfied e.g., by a system architecture document and by a hardware functional specification.

The step *threat-hazard and risk analysis* investigates safety and security requirements. First, conflicts between safety and security requirements are solved due to a specified conflict resolution approach (Fig. 7-4) including a conflict resolution policy. Such a policy defines ways of dealing with conflicts, i.e. what requirement (safety or security) to prefer in which context. This kind of requirements is influenced by the organizational safety and security policy of a project or consortium as well as the environment. A simple conflict resolution requirement would be: 'Favor safety over security.', a little more sophisticated 'Prefer functions that lead to a higher risk reduction.' At this stage of the pre-design phase a possibility is given to set the main focus of the BACS either on safety or security.

Second, the conflict resolution policy undergoes verification by actually performing the threat-hazard and risk analysis. It takes a set of safety and security requirements and measures, free from conflicts, as input. Consequences of the conflict resolution are supposed to be made obvious. The output is a list of hazards and threats and their associated risk. It has to be checked if new hazards or threats have been identified and if risk levels have been changed, respectively. Next, hazards and threats must be evaluated if they are either acceptable or not. Additionally, the risk levels are examined regarding acceptance of the degree of risk. When something is not acceptable, the conflict resolution policy has to be altered. Otherwise, the safety dependent and/or the security dependent part of the safety and security lifecycle are iterated to find new solutions to the problem, e.g. reduce SIL or EAL, revalue assets, redesign hardware architecture, and so on.

In case of having solved the conflicts, *a safety-security requirements specification* is available. It is noteworthy that from this stage on there are not any safety and security requirements, each belonging to either safety *or* security, but there are only safety-security requirements. There are requirements on the functions and measures to be implemented on an entity, requirements on the hardware and software design as well as requirements on the supporting lifecycle processes (see Fig. 5-1).

The final activity in the pre-design phase is the *safety-security requirements allocation*. The functions as well as measures and functional requirements are allocated to the hardware and software on an entity. They are input to hardware and software realization in addition to design requirements. In the end, requirements on supporting lifecycle processes are allocated and resulting in activities to be performed during the different stages of the lifecycle, e.g. style of documents or way of designing embedded software. Rigor of supporting lifecycle activities depend on the target level of safety integrity and evaluation assurance.

The document output of the pre-design lifecycle process is the safety-security requirement specification document, the safety-security plan and the validation and verification (V&V) plan as shown in Fig. 6-5. Whereas the requirement specification document is a description of what was done in the process, the latter two documents are mentioning what has to be done in all lifecycle processes.

In the style of a safety plan, standardized in [IEE12], the safety-security plan consists of the responsibilities and tasks of people involved in the development, the qualification of the staff required, methods to analyze and assess risk in the different lifecycle stages, the tool support and topics related to maintenance of documents are specified. Also the training of users, operators, maintenance and management personnel is addressed. Security related activities mentioned in the plan are mainly dealt within [ISO17]. Put succinctly, the safety-security plan covers activities of the organizational lifecycle processes. Therefore it also includes the project plan and the resources necessary to provide an adequate infrastructure for the project.

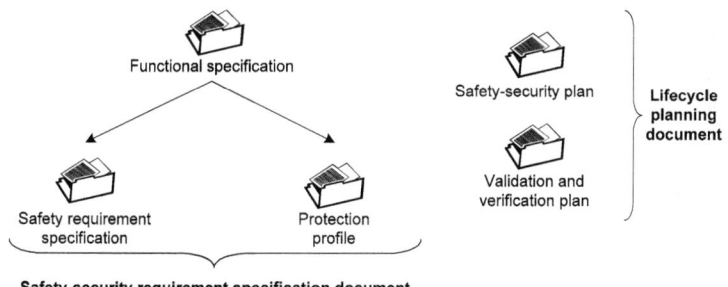

Fig. 6-5 Documents created in the pre-design process

The validation and verification (V&V) plan comprehends all activities of the supporting processes to be performed in the different primary processes in order to assess the system, entities, hardware and software, and the primary and management lifecycle activities. According to [IEE10; WRA07, pp. 33] the V&V plan lists the persons involved in the V&V process, their responsibilities, the resources, tools and techniques. Additionally, the V&V activities in the primary processes and management process are outlined. Requirements on the reporting of activities and anomalies (i.e. vulnerabilities, flaws, bugs) are given as well. Finally, the requirements are specified how to administrate the reports and how to document V&V results. A list of all documents provides an overview of the V&V results.

The safety-security requirement specification document is based on the functional specification and includes a functional description of the entity and its environment, a list of hazards and threats, security objectives, safety-security functional requirements, requirements on the supporting lifecycle processes and associated quality assurance measures, implementation independent safety-security functions, requirements on the hard- and software design and the like.

6.2 Design and Installation

The design and installation process is split up into two parts. The overall planning, installation, validation is valid for the whole BACS. In this context *overall* means looking at all the different entities in the BACS at once, i.e. a system wide view. The output from every entity lifecycle is considered to be an input to the overall activities of the system lifecycle (refer to Fig. 8-1).

The activity *realization of a safe-secure BACS entity*, however, is unique for every entity. Realization activity is divided into two portions: hardware and software realization. It includes the realization of every entity in the BACS such as a gateway and a node or even different kind of nodes. As outlined in subchapter 4.2, the Common Criteria (CC) do not mandate any typical lifecycle model. As a consequence, procedures from IEC 61508 are used and security activities according to the evaluation assurance level specified in CC are integrated.

Fig. 6-6 shows the interaction between hardware and software realization. Derived from safety-security requirements software safety-security requirements are delineated. Such requirements may be:
- Implementing a CRC with polynomial 0x12f to ensure data integrity
- Signaling data corruption to application
- Logging access of unauthorized user to an internal data table

The requirements are input to the design and development phase of software for e.g., a microcontroller on a node. A generic logic software design for a microcontroller of a node consists of three parts. The philosophy of designing safe-secure software for standard BACS is to use the standard services for data transmission and enhance it with additional functionality [REI01, pp. 31]. Finally, the software is integrated into the programmable target hardware.

1. On top is the safety-security application software.
2. The safety-security functionality is encapsulated in a software layer, i.e. firmware, and located in or above the application layer of the OSI reference model.
3. The application layer is the last layer of the standard BACS software and the base for the safety-security firmware and application software.

Software realization has to be performed in accordance with a standard software lifecycle model. These models, for example the V-model [BRO93], cover all stages in the life of software of an entity.

On the other hand, a hardware architecture for an entity is specified according to given requirements. The hardware architecture results in requirements on the programmable and non-programmable hardware. The first kinds of hardware are microcontrollers or smartcards that perform a given task implemented in software. The latter are integrated circuits such as a fail safe unit [WRA07, p. 91]. In the end, programmable hardware with software and non-programmable hardware are integrated to form a safe-secure BACS entity.

As shown in Fig. 6-6, hardware architecture is influenced by safety-security requirements. There are demands on the functionality and on the hardware design. Typically, functional requirements on the hardware are: Inputs and outputs must be testable for shortcut and stuck-at failures, power supply must be testable so that over- and under-voltage can be detected, hardware interface to a smartcard must provide a flow control.

Hardware design is very much influenced by the safety aspects, first of all by two factors: safe failure fraction (SFF) and hardware fault tolerance. Depending on the safety integrity level (SIL) a trade-off between these two factors must be found (Table 4-2). According to the target SIL, self-tests with a high diagnostic coverage must be implemented resulting in a high SFF, or (in addition) hardware redundancy is required. In the safety world always hot or active, parallel redundancy is used. That is, the redundant element is operating in the same way as the other(s) from the very beginning [BOE07, p. 146].

Common Approach

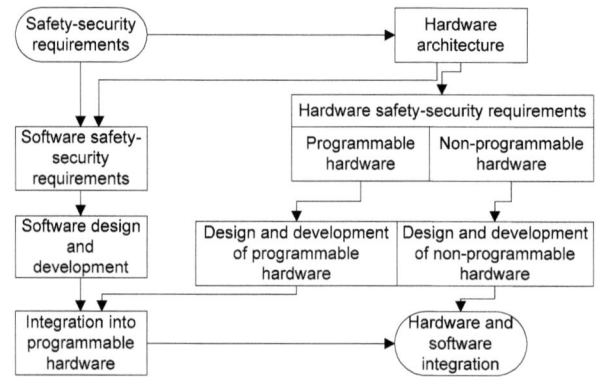

Fig. 6-6 Interaction between hardware and software realization [IEC61-2]

Hardware redundancy can result in different hardware architectures [WRA07, pp. 92; BOE07, pp. 260]. A possible architecture is the dual channel hardware architecture for entities in a BACS as shown in Fig. 6-7. It is realized in CANopen Safety or SafetyBUS p as mentioned in subchapter 3.4. A sensor value is received from Node A via the network on Node B. The sensor value is processed by the both microcontrollers and afterwards the output is set. According to the output value the actuator performs a predefined task. The two channels can cooperate or can perform actions independently.

In case of cooperation the dual channel architecture is called 1oo2 (speak: one out of two) system. From the safety point of view, in a XooY system the X stands for the number of channels required to switch to a fail safe state after a failure occurred. Y always denotes the number of channels available [WRA07, p 41]. That way of interpreting X is used in the following, since X can also be interpreted as the number of channels necessary to perform a given task.

There are two independent channels available. They perform the given task on their own. However, the actuator is only triggered if *both* channels agree. That is, the channels are AND-connected. If the channels disagree, the actuator enters a predefined fail safe state. That kind of system is not affected by a dangerous failure in one of the channels because the actuator is only triggered if both channels deliver the same result as output. Consequently, the system is tolerant towards a single fault, i.e. hardware fault tolerance of 1. In addition, such a system can be enhanced with diagnostic features. Channel 1 observes and tests channel 2 and vice versa by means of further hardware circuits. By doing so, it is possible to detect dangerous failures with software. This system is called 1oo2D where 'D' stands for diagnostic.

Even though there are 2 channels available, the 1oo2 system results in a behavior of a single channel system seen from the outside. As a consequence availability of an entity with a 1oo2 system is not increased at all, but reliability with respect to critical failures modes [KOP97] (known as safety integrity in the safety world) is raised. The entity is hardware fault tolerant in the sense of safety meaning that a hardware fault tolerance of N denotes that $N+1$ faults cause a loss of the safety status of the system. From the security point of view the entity is not fault tolerant. As stated in the Common Criteria fault tolerance means that the secure entity continues all or some of its operation despite the occurrence of failures.

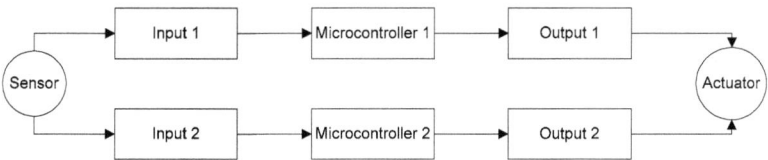

Fig. 6-7 Dual channel hardware architecture

A dual channel architecture is called 2oo2 (speak: two out of two) system when both channels are operating independently and the actuator is triggered if *just one* of the channels forces the actuator to do so. In that case the channels are OR-connected. Put succinctly, if operation in one channel fails due to a fault, the second one takes over and executes the required task. In this case redundancy through switching to a second source is applied. Such a system increases availability, but does not raise safety integrity. That is, a single dangerous failure in one of the channels is linked to a dangerous state of the complete system. From the safety perspective the hardware fault tolerance of that system is zero and it is treated like a single channel system. In the context of security, however, the fault tolerance is one and cold or unstressed redundancy is employed.

To receive – in the sense of safety – a reliable (safe hardware fault tolerance of one) and yet highly available system (secure fault tolerance of one) a three channel architecture is needed with a 2oo3 (speak: two out of three) system. Moreover, each channel consists of two outputs (*a* and *b*) [BOE04, pp. 123]. Always two outputs of different channels are AND-connected and are able to trigger the actuator. A possible connection of outputs would be: *1a* to *2a* (output 12), *1b* to *3b* (output 13) and *2b* to *3a* (output 23). A 2oo3 system is therefore comparable to three 1oo2 systems in parallel. When all three channels agree on the same value, the output is triggered. If just two of three channels deliver the same value, e.g. output 12 and output 23, the third is considered to be faulty. However, the system is still operating.

Besides the reasoning about the number of channels and as a result about the amount of microcontrollers to be deployed, it is also necessary to delve into the topic of how to access the network. Mentioned already before, quite common hardware architecture of nodes in safety related BAC systems is a two channel architecture. Hence, Fig. 6-8 shows four different ways of accessing the network always assuming a two channel architecture. Every part of the figure consists of two nodes: Node A and Node B. Each node again includes two microcontrollers (controller 1 and controller 2) and one or two network access units (NAU). The NAU are standard hardware components used to access the non-safe network. It consists of a microcontroller that handles the protocol and provides an API for the user application, and a transceiver to support the network media (powerline, twisted-pair). For example, in case of LonWorks the NAU is either a Neuron Chip [MOT97] or a LC3020 [LOY05].

The first architecture in Fig. 6-8(a) shows an architecture with two network access units, each connected to one controller. The advantage is that messages can be received independently and processed simultaneously on both controllers. In addition, a malfunction in one NAU does not result in not having access to the node. Although the safety-security functionality cannot be provided any longer, the node (if desired) can be accessed by network management tools. The level of availability is increased. As a consequence, the status of the node can be determined remotely. The drawback of such a solution is the additional hardware: two network access units are required. Moreover, each NAU is equipped with a unique network identifier (NID) in order to identify it during commissioning clearly. Hence, from a network management view a safe-secure node consists of two standard nodes because it is always assumed that one NAU comprises exactly one node. Therefore, management of the system gets even more complicated.

Fig. 6-8(b) demonstrates an architecture with only one NAU and each microcontroller is connected to the NAU. Compared to the aforementioned architecture less hardware equipment is necessary, but messages are received on both microcontrollers independently and can be processed simultaneously. The disadvantages of such an architecture are: when the NAU has a malfunction, the node cannot be accessed nor is able to send messages. Second, especially safety operations ought not to be performed on the NAU. It is a strict safety requirement that absence of reaction between NAU and microcontrollers is guaranteed. Put another way, a failure on the NAU must not affect operation on the microcontrollers at all. Therefore, its task is only to forward complete messages to the microcontrollers and receive complete messages from the microcontrollers. When both microcontrollers send a message to the NAU, both messages have to be send via the network – the same is valid for architecture (a). The NAU is not allowed to choose which one to send. As a result, bandwidth consumption is raising and additional computational power on receiver side is required since two messages have to be processed.

The third architecture illustrated in Fig. 6-8(c) mitigates problems of architecture (a) and (b). The number of hardware elements is reduced. In addition, triggering the sending process on both nodes results in a single message on the network because only one microcontroller is connected to the NAU. However, communication between the controllers is rising dramatically. Every message received must be forwarded from controller 1 to controller 2 to enable processing messages on both controllers. The same is valid for the sending process in inverse order. As mentioned before when discussing (b), a failure in the NAU results in unavailability of the node.

Fig. 6-8(d) represents a complete redundant architecture. Not only all hardware elements are duplicated, but also different networks are used. The solution includes all advantages of architecture (a) to (c), but the number of hardware elements and the two network cause additional costs.

In conclusion, there are four ways of designing the network access (Fig. 6-8) in case of a two channel architecture. At least two microcontrollers are required (c), i.e. only the controllers are duplicated. Access to the NAU as shown (b) or the NAU itself is doubled (a). Finally, two independent channels can be realized (d).

The next activity in the process is *overall planning* of installation and commissioning, safety-security validation, and operation and maintenance. The activity is influenced on the one hand by the safety-security requirements of the different entities, on the other hand by the realization of the entities. During realization of a BACS entity installation, commissioning, validation, operation and maintenance was planned for every entity. Now a system wide plan has to be created. It ensures that safety and security is not endangered during system installation or maintenance. Additionally, evaluation has to be planned to grant a specified level of safety integrity and confidence in security.

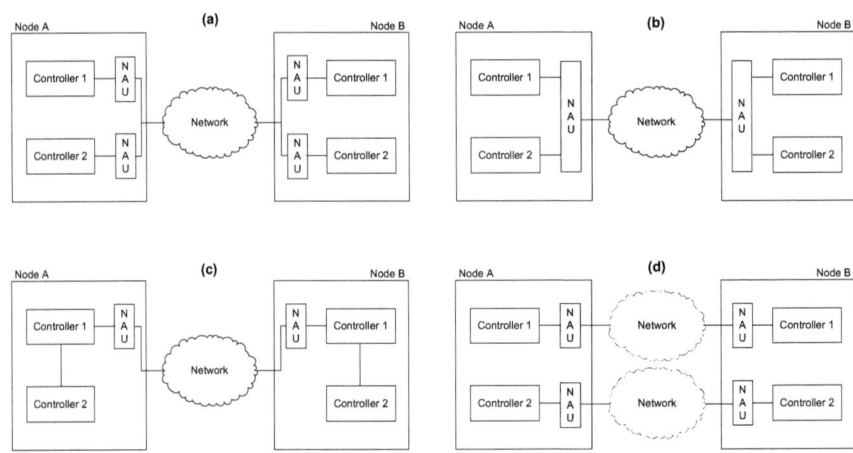

Fig. 6-8 Hardware architecture of access to the network [REI01, p. 38]

The *overall installation and commissioning* must be done in accordance with the designated plan. In general, installation and commissioning must be performed by responsible persons nominated in the plan. They have to integrate the different entities into the system as specified. It is very important that during installation and commissioning safety and security of the system is always granted. As a consequence, the following problems must be solved, specified in the plan and executed during installation and commissioning.

- A safe-secure entity must be identified clearly. A BACS may include non-safe-secure entities and safe-secure entities. Thus, authentication is required to verify the claimed identity of an entity. Not only an entity, but also the version of the firmware and type of application software must be identified unambiguously.

- Parameters to configure communication relationships must be transferred safely and securely to an entity and have to be verified by the management device. Communication parameters are used to establish logical communication paths among entities. A procedure has to be specified which guarantees that parameters sent from a management device are stored without modification on the entity. Thus, a multistage request-response mechanism may be used that returns the stored data of an entity to the management device [WRA07, pp. 191].

- Parameters to configure the application have to be sent to an entity and received safely and securely by the management device. Generally, safe-secure entities are delivered with a fixed application. Due to requirements coming from safety certification authorities, a safe-secure application cannot be uploaded with standard mechanism. Moreover, such an approach reduces the probability of installing the software in an insecure way. Uploading the software remotely leaves the possibility open for changing the software by intentional attacks without the user being able to detect it. However, parameters can be set to configure the application, for example setting timing parameters. Application parameters can be uploaded the same way as configuration parameters.

- Initial cryptographic key distribution: It is likely that safety-security measures rely on cryptographic operations (encryption, decryption). For that reason, entities that are meant to communicate have to share the same key in case of symmetric algorithms or a pair of keys in case of asymmetric algorithms. Since already the first communication among entities has to be secure, a mechanism is required that ensures secure communication from the very beginning. The requirement is mostly met by initializing entities with keys out-of-band, i.e. each entity is equipped with appropriate keys before installation. General requirements for the task are given in [IEC15-2] in family FCS_CKM.

The overall safety-security validation executes the tasks specified in the plans: overall plan, and validation and verification (V&V) plan whereas the overall validation plan can be part of the V&V plan. The activity validates the system regarding safety and security. That is, the BACS is checked against safety requirements and security objectives during its different lifecycle stages, from installation to decommissioning. Measures specified in the plan such as static tests are used to validate the system.

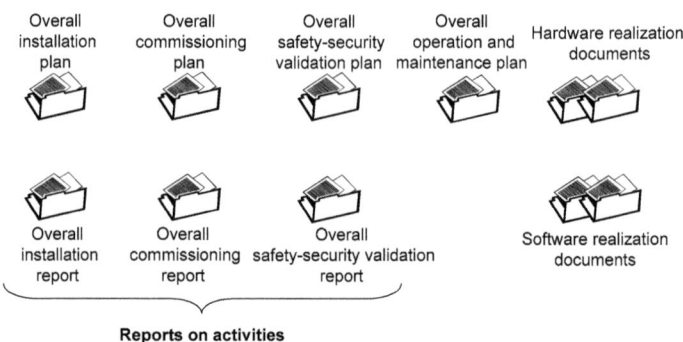

Fig. 6-9 Documents created during design and installation process

At the end of the design and installation process a great amount of new documents has been created as illustrated in Fig. 6-9: First, planning documents of the overall installation, commissioning and safety-security validation activities; second, reports on some of the planned activities; third, documents referring to hardware realization: hardware requirement specification, hardware schematics, test plans and reports; fourth, software realization documents such as software requirements specification, design document, test plan and test report.

6.3 Operation, Maintenance, Decommissioning

The last two processes, operation and maintenance, decommissioning, are summarized and dealt with in the following. Both processes relate to the use-phase of the building automation and control system (BACS). As mentioned in the introduction of subchapter 6.2, general purpose of the activities are in accordance with IEC 61508 and security relevant tasks taken from the Common Criteria are integrated.

Operation covers all activities required to operate the BACS in a safe-secure way. Therefore, the following issues should be addressed: how to test that the data transferred during commissioning was successfully stored on the designated entity; how to switch from commissioning to operation of the system; how to synchronize network time among nodes in case of applying a timestamp mechanism; how to update cryptographic keys; how to check availability of the field level network; and finally how to recover from network failures due to stochastic or systematic faults, or intentional attacks.

After the commissioning of entities (nodes, gateways) a procedure described in the overall operation and maintenance plan is required giving confidence that the configuration (communication and application related) data e.g. on a node was transferred correctly. In other words, the data stored on the management device has to be identical with the one on a node in order to guarantee a proper system behavior. Assuming that there is a safe-secure communication path between management device and node, a proper means is to use a message authentication code (MAC). Node side data is used to calculate a MAC_{Node} and the node related data is used on the management device to calculate a MAC_{Mgn_Dev}. The management device sends a request to the node asking for the MAC_{Node}. The node sends the response. In case of identical MACs ($MAC_{Mgn\_Dev} = MAC_{Node}$) it is ensured that the correct configuration data was sent to the node. Next, the management device sends a message to the node including the command to switch to operation. The aforementioned procedure must be performed for every safe-secure node.

A safety-security requirement is to detect reply, wrong sequence, delay of a message, or message insertion. A measure to detect all such network failures is to use timestamps. Such a measure, however, only works if entities communicating with each other share a common time base. In order to satisfy the requirement, a time synchronization mechanism is required. In general, two approaches are possible: a centralized time server or a decentralized approach where a pair of sender and receiver share a common time base.

In case of a centralized time synchronization approach all entities connected to the time server share the same time base. The advantage is that time management on entity side is quite simple. However, a single time server for maybe hundreds or even thousands of entities is very much susceptible for attacks. When the time server is out of order, safe-secure communication among numerous entities is not guaranteed any longer. On the contrary, the decentralized approach avoids a single point of failure, but each entity has to handle different time bases.

Which algorithm to use to synchronize time depends on the time resolution required. What most of them have in common is a request and response mechanism [IEC15, RFC43]. An entity A is sending a request to another entity B, asking for the current time. B is responding with the current time. The mechanism might be repeated [IEC58] and is applied to measure the network delay.

A lot of security measures rely on cryptographic operations. For example, a node A sends a timing request to the time server. But how can the time server be sure that the request is from the node? By means of an authentication measure the authenticity of the message can be verified. A standard security authentication measure is a message authentication code (MAC) as outlined in subchapter 1.3. Therefore, a checksum over the message is generated and ciphered with a key afterwards. The time server shares a key with node A and hence also generates the checksum and ciphers it with its key. If the MAC from the node and the time server are identical, authenticity of the message is granted.

During installation and commissioning the keys were distributed for the first time. However, keys have to be updated in a frequent manner in order to keep the data volume for cryptographic analysis limited. Moreover, they have to be updated in a secure way and not in plaintext as it is done in standard KNX/EIB with the password (refer to subchapter 3.2), and the scalability of the mechanism must be appropriate. Finally, due to the limited bandwidth at the field level symmetric keys such as [NIS46-2] are the preferred choice [NOV05, p. 21; GRA06]. Symmetric means that the same key is used to cipher and decipher data as mentioned in subchapter 1.3.

The problem of implementing an efficient key update mechanism when using symmetric keys is mostly solve by setting up a key hierarchy [RAN99, pp. 171; TRE05]. Another choice would be to store numerous different keys on a node securely at installation. The disadvantage of the latter approach is twofold: A great number of keys has to be stored because of the long lifetime of a BACS and therefore a lot of memory resources are required: A tremendous problem on node side since nodes are typical embedded devices. Second, keys have to be stored in a highly secure way. Disclosure of keys being used for operation in the future inevitably results in breaching security of the system.

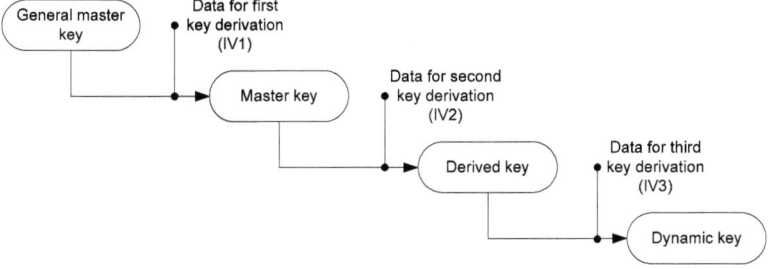

Fig. 6-10 Key hierarchy [RAN99]

In the key hierarchy (Fig. 6-10) different levels are specified and a key from a lower level is derived from a key of an upper level. Key derivation is accomplished by using a derivation function and some data changing every time a new key is derived. Such data is referred to as initialization vector (IV). [SCH01] discusses key derivation within a system wide security architecture. Derivation of a key, in turn, is performed by applying either a serial or parallel method [ABD00]. The first method uses the precedent key as initialization vector whilst the latter uses an iteration count or the current time if time synchronization is implemented as initialization vector.

As shown in Fig. 6-10, keys of a hierarchy may be implemented the following. The key at the top of the hierarchy is called general master key. The master key is derived from the general master key. The general master key and master key are stored on every entity before installation (out-of-band initialization). Dynamic keys are used for security operations. They are updated by deriving a new key from the derived key after a defined rather short timeframe. A derived key, in turn, is updated after a specified timeframe or after an attack on an asset. The keys have to be updated synchronously among the entities to grant continuous security functionality. As a consequence, update procedure can be signaled by an external master or can be performed because of the common time base among entities.

The network provides a transport service to the different entities. In particular, it enables the sensor to send its data via the network to an actuator that is acting according to the data received. The sensor 'produces' data and is called producer.

The actuator receives and 'consumes' the data and is referred to as consumer. To check the availability of the network, a producer sends messages periodically to its consumer. Such messages are called heartbeats. As long as the consumer has received heartbeats within a defined timeframe T_c, it can be sure that the network is available. When heartbeats have not been received for a period longer than T_c, unavailability of the network is assumed due to an attack or some hardware defect. Or, it is possible that the sensor has a malfunction and is not able to send heartbeats.

In case of such a failure a procedure is required that specifies how to react and recover from network failures and network attacks. In [IEC15-2] requirements are given for a trusted recovery (family FPT_RCV). For instance, after recognition of a failure the maintenance mode (fail secure state) should be entered where normal operation might be impossible or restricted. In the safety domain, such a mode is called fail safe state meaning that in the state safety of the entity is not endangered at all. Recovery can be automatic or manual. Which strategy to use depends on the failure category and has to be specified before operation. Automatic recovery means that the entity returns to normal operation after the failure disappeared, e.g. heartbeats are received again. Manual recovery requires authorized input from external. Meanwhile the entity remains in fail secure or fail safe state.

Maintenance comprises activities such as how to gather diagnostic information in order to react to failures – with respect to security related failures gathering information is called a security audit (class FAU in [IEC15-2]). Another topic is the replacement of a safe-secure entity, or modification of communication parameters. Maintenance regarding reconfiguration of a BACS in general is a very challenging task. Just think of an airport with ten thousands of nodes. It is not acceptable to shut down the complete BACS when a node shall be replaced or configuration parameters shall be changed, just because safety and security ought not to be endangered. Sophisticated management of maintenance is necessary: the impact of replacement or modification has to be analyzed by means of a hazard-threat and risk analysis.

Diagnostic information is required to react to stochastic and systematic failures, or malicious attacks. Diagnostic data comprises safety-security related events such as the number of missing heartbeats, delayed or corrupted messages, missing key updates, or attempts to access data by unauthorized entities. Next, rules have to be set up how to handle such events. For example, corrupted messages are discarded for an indefinite time. On the contrary, when a heartbeat has been missing for three times, the entity enters a fail safe state or fail secure state. The same is valid for failed key updates. In case of a reaction to a safety-security related event it can be specified to send a specific message to the management device to inform the operator about the safety-security incident. The operator, in turn, should have the possibility to access diagnostic information in a safe-secure way. Finally, diagnostic data must be stored on every entity in such a way that integrity is granted. Moreover, only authorized user ought to have access to the information.

The activity replacement as part of the maintenance process is a composition of decommissioning (the old) and installing the (new) entity. However, communication and application related parameters and cryptographic keys must be migrated from the old to the new entity. Parameters are stored in the management device as well as keys used to communicate with the new entity securely. Therefore, the following procedure can be applied. First, the old entity is switched off, replaced by the new one and the new entity is turned on and waiting for further external input. As already mentioned, each entity connected to a field level network is identified by its unique network identifier (NID). So the only difference between the two entities is the NID. Second, the new entity sends its new NID to the management device after an operator pressed a button on the entity. Third, the communication and application related parameters secured by a MAC are sent to the new device. The same procedure is applied as outlined before during operation. The MAC received and the one calculated over the parameters on the entity are compared and if equal the entity is configured properly. Fourth, the initialization vectors must be synchronized in case of using key derivation function and a key hierarchy (Fig. 6-10).

Modification of communication related parameters is always required when the logical or physical network topology is reconfigured, for example a new entity is added or new sensors are connected to a node. Second, changing communication related parameters also results in establishing new safe-secure paths, i.e. keys have to be exchanged among the new entities. As mentioned in subchapter 2.1, BACS is a rather dynamic system and thus the topic modification must be considered.

Adding a new entity to the system, i.e. reconfigure the physical network topology, requires tasks equal to the ones described in the replacement activity when installing a new entity. Changing the logical network topology is always triggered by the management device and either a parameter is added or deleted. Inserting a new logic communication path is identical to the procedure outlined during installation, deleting equivalent to decommissioning.

Decommissioning is the last stage of the safety-security lifecycle. There are three ways of understanding decommissioning: The whole system, an entity or a logical communication path can be decommissioned. The first and the second type require the third type described in the following. First, all the logical communication parameters of an entity are deleted. Second, the entity is turned off. The procedure is repeated with every entity and finally the system is decommissioned.

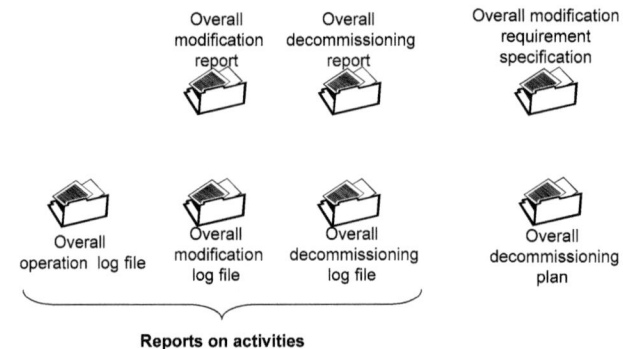

Fig. 6-11 Documents created during installation and maintenance, and decommissioning process

Deletion of communication related parameters on entity A has an impact on other entities (B, C ...) logically connected to A. For a better understanding, let's assume the following scenario. Node A receives sensor data from Node B and Node C. In addition, Noda A sends sensor data to Node D. Put another way, Node A is a consumer and 'consumes' information from producers B and C and 'produces' information for Node D. Communication parameter is deleted on Node A so that no more data is accepted from B and C. Moreover, communication parameters in B and C are deleted that were used to send data to A. In the end, it has to be verified in order to ensure the integrity of system communication, first that parameters on A, B, and C were deleted and second that deletion process had no impact on logical communication between Node A and Node D. As a consequence, the same procedure as described when discussing installation is used. The management device calculates a MAC over the communication parameters of every Node. Each node does the same using its parameters. If every MAC of Node A, B, C, and D is identical with the one from the management device, decommissioning was successful and integrity guaranteed.

Documents of the use-phase (Fig. 6-11) are separated in requirement specification and plan, i.e. cover what to do and reports and log files. The reports outline the tasks performed whereas the log files gives information on the tasks in chronological order.

7. Key Ideas of Common Approach

In chapter 6, a common approach used to develop a safe-secure BACS was presented. The common approach is based on the lifecycle standardized in IEC 61508 and the security concept of IEC 15408 (Common Criteria) is integrated similar to the approach presented in [SCH05]. It specifies four primary processes (Fig. 5-2) as they are incorporated in typical generic lifecycle models.

In the following the common approach is discussed with focus on the topics that are new and proposed by the author, i.e. to use *such* a lifecycle model and to harmonize safety and security. In addition, it is explained why safety is investigated first in the pre-design phase and what safety-security validation means. Another topic corresponds to the relationship between safety and security: a way of conflict resolution between safety and security requirements as well as safety and security measure assessment are presented.

7.1 Safety-security Lifecycle

The term *lifecycle model* was already outlined in general in subchapter 2.2 and in the introduction in chapter 4. A detailed definition of lifecycle model is given in [IEC12]: "A framework containing the processes, activities, and tasks involved in the development, operation, and maintenance […], spanning the life of the system from the definition of its requirements to the termination of its use." The advantage of a lifecycle model is the formal and structured way of development, operation and maintenance because requirements on the processes, activities and tasks are given for every stage in the system life.

Within the thesis lifecycle is an umbrella term for every model that covers all stages in the life of a system. Therefore arrows in Fig. 6-1 need not to symbolize a sequential development progress, such as the waterfall model [ROY70] does. Activities are not necessarily integrated into the lifecycle as instance, but mostly as iteration [IEE17] as mentioned in subsection 5.2.2. Arrows in the safety-security lifecycle imply that tasks of activity *n* requires input from the preceding activity *n-1* and delivers an output to the following activity *n+1*. Activity *n* is considered to be finished when all activity input is processed and the complete specified output is available.

As shown in Fig. 7-1, an activity of the lifecycle needs four pieces of input information and generates three pieces of output information. In case of an instance, all input information is available and the whole output information can be generated at once. By contrast, in case of an iteration only some pieces of input information are available at first, and step by step further input information is existing to finally receive all required output information.

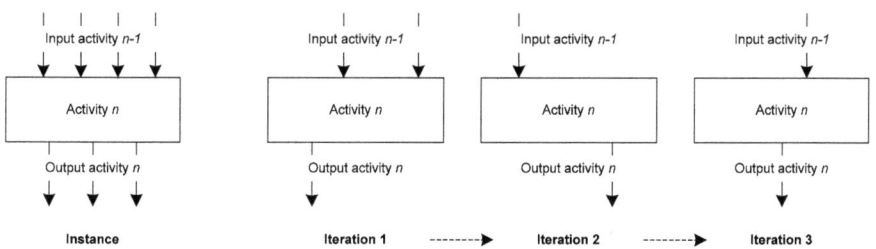

Fig. 7-1 Mapping of activities in a lifecycle

7.1.1 Motivation

Safety and security issues ought to be considered not only during requirement specification, but also during design, operation, maintenance and decommissioning. Hence, a lifecycle model is used as 'development-use' model in the common approach. The reasons are the following.

1. Safety is concerned with ensuring systematic and hardware integrity (see subchapter 4.1). Therefore measures are necessary to avoid and detect faults in order to minimize risk to people. Stochastic failures endanger hardware integrity. They occur during the use-phase and can only be detected, not avoided. On the contrary, systematic failures jeopardize systematic integrity

during development- and use-phase. They can be avoided during development and detected during use-phase.

2. Security deals with minimizing risk to assets coming from threats and vulnerabilities (see subchapter 4.2). Countermeasures are threat and vulnerability avoidance, and threat control. The first is only possible during development whilst threat control is performed during use-phase.

3. A BACS consists of many entities such as nodes, gateways, management devices and so on. Due to the large number of nodes as mentioned in subchapter 1.1, clearly defined requirements for the use-phase are of great importance. E.g., how to install and maintain the system safely and securely.

As mentioned in subchapter 5.2, various lifecycle models, in particular for safety, also some for security are available in literature. [IEE10] specifies requirements on how to develop a (software project) lifecycle. It might seem reasonable to develop a completely new lifecycle because a new field of application is entered. And ideas of models in literature are used as input.

Special focus, however, is paid to the acceptance of the common approach by safety experts and security practitioners as mentioned in subchapter 2.1. Furthermore, the common approach shall allow for certification of products. In the end, it shall specify a level of safety and security to compare products. As a consequence, reinventing the wheel and developing a new lifecycle is the wrong choice as mentioned in [SCH05]. The solution is to use a well approved standardized lifecycle – the one in IEC 61508 [IEC61]. The standard is a generic standard for functional safety and it explicitly means to allow development of domain and application specific standards. IEC 61508 also specifies four levels, so called safety integrity levels (SIL), that make a comparison of different product possible. Safety integrity levels are defined by different numbers of failure probability per hour (Table 4-1).

Security issues are covered by IEC 15408 [IEC15] because it gives requirements for the various stages in the system life too. Moreover, it specifies a level of security: seven evaluation assurance levels (EAL). Evaluation assurance levels specify a set of requirements from the different assurance classes (Table 4-3). IEC 15408, however, does not mandate any specific 'development-use' model. As a result, the safety-security lifecycle uses the model presented in IEC 61508 and integrates security related issues. Additional activities are specified to cover the topics resulting from the interaction of safety and security, such as conflict resolution or measure assessment (see subchapter 7.2).

Noteworthy to say, the measurands SIL and EAL are different in their definition. Both levels, however, have in common that the higher the level the more and stricter requirements must be met. A higher level results in a higher risk reduction. And products shall be compared regarding their ability to reduce risk to a defined level.

7.1.2 Macro- and Micro-Processes

The safety-security lifecycle specifies activities for the different processes in the lifecycle of a system, the building automation and control system (BACS). The word *overall* in Fig. 6-1 intends that the complete BACS is meant. Put another way, the safety-security lifecycle gives requirements for macro-processes, i.e. how to development and use the BACS. Nodes, gateways or management devices are subsystems, each consisting of hardware or software, or both. The safety-security lifecycle is used for subsystems also and called entity lifecycle. That is, various entity lifecycles comprise the system lifecycle (Fig. 7-2, Fig. 8-1). Subsystems can be created for a specific system or already existing third party subsystems might be integrated into a new BACS. As a consequence, overall planning is influenced by the requirements in case of new subsystems to be developed otherwise by the realization of the subsystem.

Software engineering and hardware development is performed in accordance with well established models: the V-model [BRO93], the spiral model [BOE88], the incremental model [BAL98] or the like for software realization. Processes giving requirements on hardware and software engineering are called micro-processes.

Macro- and micro processes can further be distinguished between primary, and supporting and organizational processes according to [IEC12]. In addition, processes consist of several activities. In the safety-security lifecycle an activity corresponds with an enumerated stage in Fig. 6-1.

Primary Processes

Primary processes in [IEC12] are acquisition, supply, development, operation and maintenance process as outlined in subchapter 5.2. The safety-security lifecycle, however, includes the pre-design, design and installation, operation and maintenance, and decommissioning process as primary processes. The reason for specifying the aforementioned four processes is that the target audiences of the common approach are developer, operator and maintainer as mentioned in subchapter 2.3. Therefore no explicit processes for acquisition and supply are defined, but more emphasis is laid on development and use of the system.

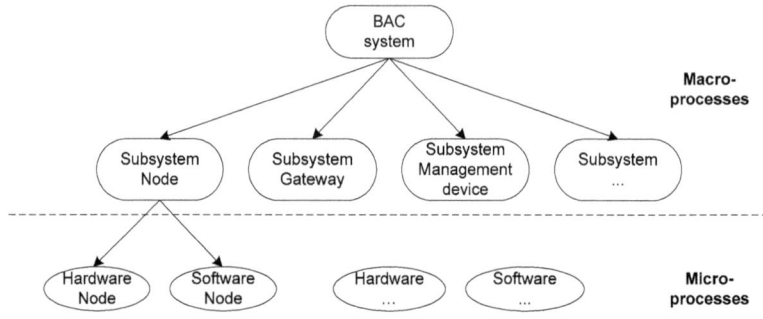

Fig. 7-2 Lifecycle macro- and micro-processes

Primary processes, and their activities and tasks are directly relating to the development and use of the system. Moreover, they invoke supporting and organizational processes. I.e., the activity 'overall safety and security validation' invokes the supporting activity 'validation' and 'documentation'. In contrast to the approaches presented in [FIR03] or [POO05], safety and security related activities are not considered to be independent supporting processes. They are embedded explicitly into the primary processes to emphasize their importance and to highlight the objective of the common approach: development and use of a safe-secure BACS.

Supporting and Organizational Processes

Supporting lifecycle processes support another process as an integral part in order to raise the quality and contribute to the success of the project. Moreover, organizational processes are established by an organization as an underlying structure for associated lifecycle processes.

Organizational processes at project level according to [IEC12] are the management process, managing the supporting processes; the infrastructure process establishing the required infrastructure; at organizational level the improvement process assessing an improving processes and the training process providing and maintaining trained personnel. In accordance with [IEC12], supporting lifecycle processes are the documentation, configuration management, quality assurance (verification, validation, joint review, audit) and problem resolution process.

These processes force to evolve a safety-security culture in a project. Activities of the processes make a contribution to the success of a project by assuring a level of safety integrity and of confidence in security. Rigor of lifecycle process activities depends on the safety integrity level (SIL) and evaluation assurance level (EAL). The higher the levels the more attention is paid to supporting lifecycle activities. It is important to point out that developing and using a safe-secure BACS does not only mean to meet all technical requirements. Therefore, functional safety management is introduced in the safety domain [WRA07, pp. 25]. In [MCG06] something equivalent is presented for security: software security – best practice to engineer software with paying attention to the security situation through the whole software lifecycle.

7.1.3 Safety First

As shown in Fig. 6-1, the lifecycle model starts with activities related to safety. Output of the activities is used as input to security related activities. Finally, pre-design phase ends with activities linked to safety and security. In [EAM99] safety and security issues are investigated independently. At the end of specification safety and security requirements are only cross-checked regarding conflicts. In [STO06] a risk framework for safety and security is discussed: Security threats are seen as input to the safety risk framework. They are considered as safety hazards that lead to risk. Refer to subchapter 5.1 for the details on [EAM99] and [STO06].

The safety-security lifecycle, however, starts with activities referring to safety and then investigates security issues. This procedure was chosen because [OVA07]:

1. IEC 61508 specifies a very strict and formal way of receiving requirements. The IEC 61508 approach is very well adopted and often a legal requirement. Therefore, it is very likely that a well described input is given to the activities related to security. In turn, quality of security related activities is going to be raised.

2. Depending on the safety integrity level a hardware fault tolerance different from zero is required (see Table 4-2). This requirement results in a specific

physical subsystem architecture of an entity, e.g. 1oo2 architecture that must be taken into consideration while establishing the security environment.

3. Depending on the chosen safety integrity level (SIL) defined activities of supporting lifecycle processes to ensure quality during the *whole* lifecycle are specified. Whereas security assurance requirements in an evaluation assurance package of a defined evaluation assurance level (EAL) only specify such activities to be performed *after the pre-design phase*. Activities to grant a level of quality during pre-design phase are always the same, regardless of the EAL.

4. Moreover, assets to be protected including safety requirements might comprise the security environment. In most BAC systems safety is a key application functionality that cannot be readjusted.

Since it is possible that security requirements influence safety issues in a negative way, threat-hazard and risk analysis allows for cross-checking safety and security requirements. The activity is a means to verify whether security requirements jeopardize safety targets. If so, stages in the lifecycle must be repeated in an iterative way to finally receive a complete set of safety-security requirements.

7.1.4 Safety-security Functions

The output of the pre-design phase in the safety-security lifecycle (Fig. 6-1) is a set of safety-security functions having been allocated to hardware or software. They are implementation independent and are seen as constraints to be taken into account when specifying the general hardware and software requirements. General means that not only safety-security functionality is considered, but all the non-safety-security related functionality necessary to get the entity performing as expected. On the contrary to software requirements engineering [POO05, FIR03], safety-security functions are not supporting the primary functionality by imposing quality attributes on the system, but they are the primary functionality.

Let's assume a safe-secure node as example, consisting of two microcontrollers (1oo2 hardware architecture). Every microcontroller has an interface to a smartcard used to store secret data such as cryptographic keys. Messages sent over the network are created by both microcontrollers. They are compared and if they are identical sent to another node. Some messages might be encrypted or authenticated with a key. This operation is performed on the smartcard. Received messages are processed by both microcontrollers and if both agree on the integrity and if necessary on the authenticity, the payload of the message is considered to be valid. A safety-security function is 'encryption/decryption of data' and 'data authentication'.

General hardware requirements are: 'a serial interface between microcontrollers' and 'a serial interface to every smartcard.' Otherwise, an agreement on the integrity and authenticity of a message between both microcontrollers would not be possible. Derived from the hardware requirements, a software requirement is: 'a serial driver and an API to handle serial communication'. Additionally, payload of messages received is going to be processed by an application. Another software requirement is 'forward payload received in an message to the application'.

Even though function specification is part of the design phase in a generic lifecycle, safety-security function specification is part of the pre-design phase. The type of function specification is looked on as a constraint to be considered during design of an entity in the BACS.

7.1.5 Validation and Verification

Validation as well as verification is defined as a process of *evaluating* a system as already mentioned in subchapter 2.2. Verification is a process performed after every activity of a lifecycle process to determine if the output coming from the activity satisfies conditions imposed at the start of the activity [IEE74]. Moreover, according to [IEE10] verification deals with giving evidence of conformance to requirements, and adherence to standards, practices, conventions during lifecycle processes, and giving evidence of successful completion of each lifecycle activity. Verification means asking the question: 'Are we building the system correctly?'

In the safety-security lifecycle (Fig. 6-1), verification process to prove conformance to lifecycle process requirements (Fig. 5-1) is not mentioned explicitly because it has to be executed without exception after every activity in the lifecycle. For example, stage 8 of the safety-security lifecycle, security requirements specification, has the goal to specify security related requirements. Verification means to check that every security objective is at least implemented by one security requirement. Additionally, verification is carried out at the end of hardware and software development. E.g., it has to be checked that the source code, considered to be the output of software development, conforms to the software requirements, i.e. to portions of the system requirements (Fig. 5-1). The latter type of verification is mentioned explicitly in the hardware or software lifecycle because it is not performed regularly.

In [IEE74] validation is a process carried out during or at the end of development in order to determine if specified requirements are met. Additionally, in [IEE10] validation is considered to be the process that checks if system requirements are satisfied, the right problem is solved and the indented use is satisfied. In other words, validation means checking the system behavior against its intended use: 'Are we building the right system?'

Validation activity regarding safety-security is mentioned explicitly because it is not performed periodically in contrast to the lifecycle process requirement verification. In the field of safety (IEC 61508) the summary of safety requirements is considered to be the specification of intended use and system requirements (Fig. 7-3). Therefore, safety validation is the process of comparing system behavior with the safety requirements specification(s). In the context of security (IEC 15408), security objectives are a statement of indent (Fig. 7-3). In addition, an assurance technique is a means used to produce confidence that an entity meets its security objectives. And, evaluation gives evidence of assurance. Evaluation in [IEC15-1] has two aspects: validating the protection profile(s) including the security objectives and verification of the conformance of the system with its functional and assurance requirements. Security validation is therefore refers to checking the system against the security objectives (Fig. 7-3).

In conclusion, seen from a more general point of view safety-security validation is concerned with investigating if risks have been mitigated properly and risk mitigation strategy is working. Testing techniques as described in [IEC61] or [IEC15-3] can be used to ensure the effectiveness of risk mitigation strategy.

How to proceed during validation and verification process is written down in the V&V plan, also what measures have to be used. Results of validation and verification is noted in reports. The documents are referenced in the V&V plan. Typical measure to check the process requirements are static techniques like reviews (inspection or walk-through), to check the system requirements dynamic techniques like black box or white box testing [IEC61-7] are applied. Validation regarding safety-security either uses dynamic techniques like simulation or static techniques such as static analysis.

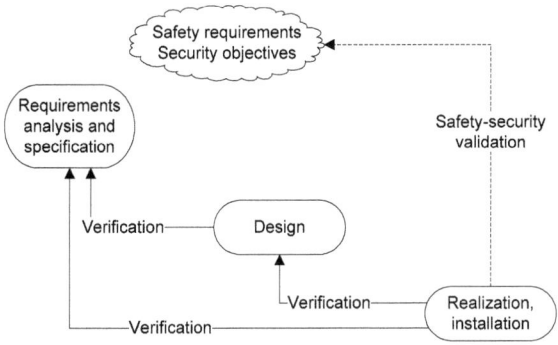

Fig. 7-3 Safety-security validation and verification process

7.2 Relationship between Safety and Security

Safety and security more or less interact in every stage of the lifecycle. Both either show identities or conflicts. Of course, there are also topics where they do not interact. The requirements are considered to be independent. Identity means that safety and security strive for the same with equal or different effort. In opposite to identity, conflict indicates that safety and security pursue contradicting things.

Conflicts or identities between safety and security are always a result of conflicting or identical requirements. Consequently, to figure out and resolve conflicts between safety and security requirements, it is necessary to examine interdependencies. That is why activity threat-hazard and risk analysis is integrated into the pre-design phase of the lifecycle (Fig. 6-1, stage 9).

After stage 8 of the pre-design process safety requirements were specified that are part of the security environment. Additionally, a set of security requirements is available already considering safety requirements. What is still missing at this point is a crosschecking of both sets of requirements. Are the safety and security requirements complementary? Do security requirements contradict safety requirements and vice versa? Therefore, the conflict resolution approach in Fig. 7-4 is applied. The result is a conflict free set of requirements. Next, the measures implemented to satisfy the conflict free requirements are checked. Only these measures are crosschecked that are different although they result from the same requirement, stated once during safety and a second time during security requirement specification. After measures assessment has been performed, the threat-hazard and risk analysis is carried out to verify the correctness of the decisions made during conflict resolution and measure assessment. Especially, the conflict resolution policy is checked if it delivers the appropriate result with regard to the field of application of the BACS.

7.2.1 Conflict Resolution Approach

Even though safety and security have the same major goal, namely risk reduction, they reduce risk because of different reasons. Put succinctly, safety is concerned with reducing risk to people, whereas security strives for minimizing risk to information and resources. Refer to subchapter 1.2 and 1.3 for detailed definition. Accordingly, it is very likely that requirements how to reduce risk differ. Even worse, it is almost inevitable that these requirements contradict each other. Hence, a methodology has to be specified that presents a clear and concise, and easy to handle way of conflict resolution. Such an approach is shown in Fig. 7-4. It consists of two parts: a separation of requirements into two groups to perform the conflict resolution itself afterwards.

Resolving requirements conflicts has already been discussed extensively in the software engineering domain. In [LAM98] the problem is addressed and a methodology called KAOS is used to manage conflicts. A formal way of dealing with conflicts is proposed, not covering safety and security problems explicitly. [POO05] discusses a means, called non-functional decomposition (NFD), to resolve requirement conflicts. It separates requirements into primary and supplementary requirements. Security requirements are explicitly mentioned and are only considered to be supplementary requirements. Integration of safety and security requirements and resulting conflicts are addressed in [ZAF05]. Safety and security are integrated in the form of integrated behavior tree and step by step refined into a design behavior tree giving a so called design behavior view of the system. The view provides a platform for requirements conflict resolution.

What the three approaches in particular and approaches in the field of software engineering in general have in common, is a very formal and often abstract way of dealing with the problem of conflict resolution. Additionally, all the approaches of course are dedicated to software. As outlined in subchapter 2.2, the common approach should be accepted by safety and security experts. They are used to rules, accustomed to explicit stated requirements on how to develop, used to 'best practice'. As a consequence, the conflict resolution approach specified in the following is based on predefined rules that are applied to solve a conflict. Such a way of handling conflicts is also understandable for BACS developers and integrators.

A list of safety and security requirements is available after stage 8 of the pre-design process (Fig. 6-1). As stated before, they can be independent, identical or conflicting. To solve the conflict among requirements, a conflict resolution policy has to be applied. It should state a set of rules how to deal with conflicting safety and security requirements. Such rules are specified with regard to the field of application, the organizational safety and security policies and the operational environment. According to the rules conflicting requirements are evaluated and either the safety or the security one is discarded.

The conflict resolution policy enables the developer to allow for the particular point of view of course. As mentioned in [BUR92], it is absolutely reasonable to view a BACS and its entities as being security or safety critical or both. From a system point of view for example, a room in a building is equipped with a climate control that heats or cools the room. Inside a server is placed that stores credit cards numbers of thousands of customers. If the climate control is compromised in summer, the temperature in the room rises and the server crashes. Availability of the server does not exist any more. Therefore the system is considered to be security critical. Just imagine, though, that inside the room a patient is lying in his bed, unable to move because of a car accident. The climate control fails and decreases the temperature of the room continuously and therefore endangers the life of the patient. Thus the system represents a safety critical one.

It must be mentioned that it is not always easy to classify a system or subsystem and its entities to be either security or safety critical. Thinking about the example given before, it is possible that many rooms with patients are available like in a hospital. Nodes of three rooms are grouped in a domain and domains are connected via gateways. The system can be accessed remotely by means of a remote entity via a so called remote gateway. The remote entity is used to manage the system and uses a safe-secure message format to send messages to the entities of the BACS. As stated before, the complete system is considered to be safety critical, but the remote gateway is security critical because of the following reason. It is assumed that the remote gateway is the virtual entrance to the BACS and therefore checks the access to the BACS by having implemented an access control. From the safety point of view this entity is transparent assuming that it does not interpret the payload of the message. In that case it only forwards messages.

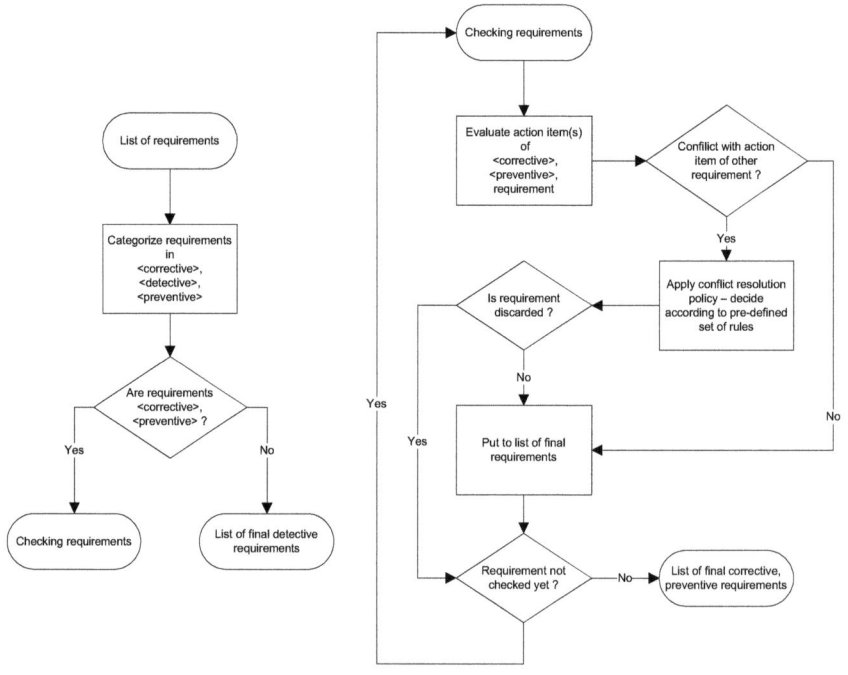

Fig. 7-4 Conflict resolution approach

Consequently, the conflict resolution policy can specify rule(s) valid for a system or subsystem. E.g., 'Safety requirements are preferred because the system is considered to be safety-critical.' A more detailed policy focuses on the different entities and network types. A BACS may include gateways among domains or nodes with different computational power and memory resources. So there might be policies for every entity; for the residual gateway and a node in a server room one preferring security, other favoring safety requirements. In case of conflicting requirements allocated to software, a conflict resolution policy may be specified for the firmware and another for the application software. The policy for the firmware will correspond to the intention of the BACS in general. If the intention of the BACS is to be used in a hospital, conflict resolution policy will tend to prefer safety requirements rather than security ones. One of the many applications in a hospital is the control of a door giving access to a room where drugs are stored. Conflict resolution for such application software is favoring security requirements.

Following the conflict resolution specification, each safety and security requirement is categorized. In general, a requirement is specified to reach a defined objective. As mentioned in subchapter 4.1, the objectives of safety is to guarantee hardware and systematic integrity by fault avoidance during the different phases of the lifecycle and fault control (detection and correction) during operation of the system [IEC61-2]. Security is concerned with preventing and mitigating the loss of confidentiality, integrity and availability [IEC15-1]. Although the naming is different, safety and security objectives are prevention, detection and correction. Hence three types of categories of safety and security requirements are specified as shown in Fig. 7-5 [HER03, p. 85]. It is noteworthy that requirements can fall into more than one category.

1. Preventive: An objective of every safety and security system is to prevent faults or attacks. In the safety world that objective is called fault avoidance – other wording, but same meaning. A typical preventive objective is 'Documentation will be available and managed by a document administration program.'. Consequently, a requirement is 'Software architecture is documented and stored in a document database.'.

2. Detective: Safety and security systems aim at detecting faults and attacks. For example, 'The loss of system data integrity will be detect.' As a result, a requirement is 'Integrity of system data is detected.'.

3. Corrective: Such an objective delineates the corresponding response to a fault or an attack, i.e. the action to be taken. E.g., 'In case of failure the node will return to a known state'. A derived requirement says, 'A known state is specified when a failure occurs'.

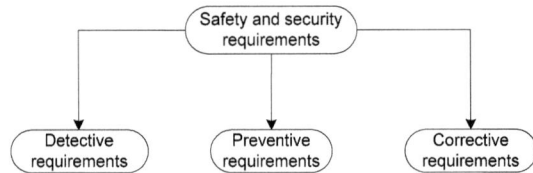

Fig. 7-5 Classes of requirements

Detective requirements result in actions that monitor the processes or the system during the different stages of the lifecycle. For example, every message is checked regarding data integrity. A possible loss of integrity due to a stochastic failure or intentional attack is detected. How to react in case of loss of integrity is specified by a corrective requirement. Safety and security requirements of the category detective requirements are identical, supporting or independent because they are just monitoring and therefore not influencing the processes or system itself. However, countermeasures, i.e. implementation of activities, may differ and are subject to discussion in subchapter 7.2.2.

A conflict between safety and security requirements is possible if actions are derived from a corrective or preventive object. A corrective and preventive requirement specifies actions and a reaction to an incident. These types of actions are influencing the process or system. Especially, corrective requirements have to be investigated regarding conflicts. They determine actions of how to respond to and recover from a failure or attack. In other words, corrective requirements lead to actions to be executed under abnormal circumstances. Conflicts may occur because the intention of safety – reduce risk to people – and security – reduce risk to resources – differ. A simple and classic example is a door. Under normal circumstances the door opens and closes when an authorized person wants to enter the room. If it is opened, it should be guaranteed that the person is not hurt. So also safety is involved. In case of a failure, i.e. under abnormal circumstances, it is not clear what the state of the door is. The reaction of the system can be either to open or close the door according to the specified conflict resolution policy.

After a list of corrective and preventive requirements is available, each requirement is evaluated regarding its action item (Fig. 7-4). That is, the action and the reaction to a failure or attack are evaluated. The action item is checked against the other action items of corrective or preventive requirements. If there is no conflict, the requirement is considered to be a final safety-security requirement. Otherwise, the conflict resolution policy is applied and one of the requirements is discarded. In the end, a conflict-free set of requirements exists that undergoes verification by a threat-hazard and risk analysis as presented in subchapter 6.1.

7.2.2 Measure Assessment

In general, it has to be distinguished between functional and non-functional measures. The latter are often called quality assurance measures. The intention of the measures is to raise the level of quality of the system. They are means used to implement activities of the supporting and organizational lifecycle processes. In the context of safety and security they provide support in order to reach a defined level of safety integrity and confidence in security. As shown in Fig. 7-6 [FRU02, p. 25], the measures can be divided into three classes.

Fig. 7-6 Quality assurance measures

1. *Design* measures are used to avoid faults or detect them at a very early stage in the development and are therefore preventive measures. Typical examples are the use of a 'development-use' model, a configuration management system or development tools, or project management activities.

2. *Analytical* measures check the system (tests and reviews), the processes (audit) and observe and measure the system. Checks can either by dynamic or static such as code walkthroughs. Dynamic checks are black-box or white-box tests.

3. *Organizational* measures are supporting design and analytical measures. Examples are the use of standardized concepts described in national or interna-

tional standards, training of employees or management of the technical infrastructure, guidelines and checklists.

Functional measures are the implementation of functions whereas functions are derived from requirements. Such measures are sometimes called methods or techniques too. Functional safety-security measures are implemented in hardware or software on an entity in the BACS, such as a node or a gateway. Typical functional measures are cyclic redundancies check (CRC) or a hash algorithm or software monitoring.

One of the many motivations to design a common approach is to benefit from synergies on applying measures. Safety and security measures and synergies gained can be classified in three groups [OVA07]. Since the thesis is focused on the hard- and software of a node of a BACS, measure assessment is outlined for functional measures only. It is assumed that the same procedure can be applied to assess quality assurance measures.

1. There are measures that *directly match* derived from the same or different requirements. The safety as well as security requirement 'Detect delay and loss of a message' results in the measure 'Use of timestamps or sequence numbers for delayed or repeated messages'. Or, the safety requirement 'Detect systematic software failures' and the security requirement 'Detect deliberate corruption of security related software' lead to the measure 'Use of the online self tests walking pattern [HOE86, pp. 7-56]'. Usually there is not going to be a problem to commonly use them. Therefore, high potential for synergies exists since measures are easily combinable.

2. There are measures that are *unique* for safety and security and need to be implemented separately. Consequently, no synergies are possible. E.g., a security requirement is 'Avoid disclosure of sensitive data' and therefore 'Use a confidentiality measure'. A safety requirements can be 'Detect shortcut of cable to external sensor on node side ' and hence 'Use of test pulses'.

3. There are measures that require *different efforts*, e.g. in terms of computational power or consumed memory, although they are derived from the same requirement. A common safety and security requirement may be 'Integrity of network related data must be ensured'. The safety measure is 'Use of a 2 byte CRC (cyclic redundancy check)' whilst the security measure is 'Use of

a 16 byte MAC (message authentication code)'. Both of these measures protect the integrity of the message, but the execution time (e.g., 10-100µs for CRC and 8-15ms for MAC) and memory resource (e.g., length 2 byte for CRC and 16 byte for MAC) differ.

Measure assessment has to be only performed when safety and security measures are of group 3: different measures with different effort are derived from the same requirement. Just that group of measures exhibit conflicts regarding e.g., computational power, throughput, computation time, memory resources or application constraints. Measures of the other groups are either identical or unique and thus cannot be conflicting per definition.

Assessment of measures derived from functions and the associated requirements is influenced by six factors (Fig. 7-7) including a safety and security related one. Factor 1-3 were already investigated during stage 2 and stage 5 of the safety-security lifecycle (Fig. 6-1).

Field of application. Building automation services in general are not real-time critical. That is, reaction times within a couple of microseconds are not of concern. Standard HVAC services require reaction times within minutes. The same for smoke detection service or a security alert service. An emergency push button application used to stop a revolving door, however, needs a reaction time within some hundreds of milliseconds.

Hardware environment. Measures are dependent on the deployed hardware. The memory resources, computational power or interfaces provided must be considered. Typically, nodes are embedded systems with limited resources whereas gateways are equipped with more resources compared to nodes. Additionally, the performance of the network must be taken into account. Field level networks are low bandwidth, backbone level networks are generally high bandwidth ones.

Software environment. The safety-security related software includes different measures and may interface with other non-safety-security related software such as an operating system or an API (application programming interface). That kind of software is a constraint to be taken into consideration.

Safety integrity level (SIL) specifies the level of performance of a safety function and the associated measure. In the context of safety, performance essentially means the likelihood of carrying out the adequate action(s), e.g. detecting faults. The SIL is applicable to all kinds of measures. Moreover, measures used to detect stochastic faults such as online self tests are characterized by their diagnostic coverage (DC).

Evaluation assurance level (EAL) is a security related factor. The EAL defines a scale for measuring assurance and includes individual assurance components varying in depth and rigor depending on the level. One assurance component is strength of function (SOF): It specifies the minimum effort assumed to defeat the security behavior by directly attacking the associated functional measure. In other words, it defines the security performance of a measure. SOF attribute is only applicable to permutational functional measures like hash functions.

Performance. EAL and SIL are covering safety and security performance: likelihood of detect faults or effort to break a security function. Performance in the context refers to topics like throughput, reaction time, computational power and memory resources required.

Generally, functional measures differ in the kind of realization and performance. As mentioned before, functional measures are realized either in hardware or software. Consequently, they very likely interact with hardware and software, respectively. That is, the reason why the hardware and software environment has to be investigated. These functional measures provide various functionalities that differ in terms of performance. In the context performance means throughput, reaction time, but also safety and security performance. Necessary reaction time, throughput and so on is dependent on the field of application. Finally, safety and security performance is specified by the safety integrity and evaluation assurance levels.

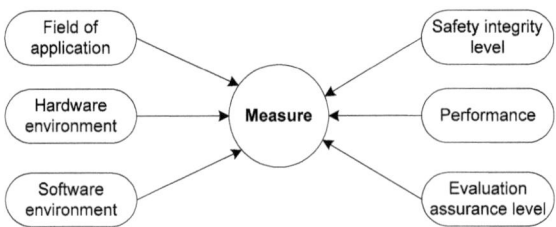

Fig. 7-7 **Factors used to assess measures**

Before giving an example, it is outlined why measure assessment need not necessarily apply the same policy used during conflict resolution (see subchapter 7.2.1). It would be possible to simply use safety related measures if conflict resolution policy favors safety or implement security related measures in case of security being preferred in the policy. Moreover, it would make sense because conflict resolution policy is influenced by quite the same factors. During conflict resolution at requirement level, however, no attention is paid to the implementation of the functions derived from the requirements. Although safety and security performance (SIL and EAL) are considered in the conflict resolution policy, performance regarding throughput, computational power, timing, reaction time is not taken into consideration. Performing measure assessment independently of conflict resolution does not exclude applying security measures in safety critical scenarios and vice versa. Especially, implementing security measures in safety critical environments adds additional value to the system. That is, because security related measures (also) withstand intentional attacks on the contrary to safety related ones.

Next, an example is give of how to assess measures. In the safety world it is common practice to send 'alive messages', so called heartbeats, between a producer (sensor) and a consumer (actuator). They are sent periodically to check whether the network is still available and messages are not misdirected on their way from the producer to the consumer. Additionally, it gives the consumer evidence that the producer is still operating. Heartbeats must be protected from stochastic failures on the network. Furthermore, since a consumer should just accept heartbeats from particular defined producers, an access control is required.

Safety measures are on the one hand source based addresses to avoid insertion of messages. They are used to some kind of authenticate a heartbeat to be allowed to access the consumer. Moreover a CRC is in use to ensure integrity of the heartbeat. The source based addressing model says that every producer is assigned a safe address. Every consumer holds a table with the safe addresses of producers. Only if the safe address of the producer in the heartbeat is in the table on consumer side, the heartbeat is accepted. A security measure ensuring integrity and authenticity of a heartbeat is the message authentication code (MAC). Producer and consumer share a symmetric key or pair of asymmetric keys. Producer appends the MAC ciphered with the key and the consumer checks the MAC by deciphering the MAC. If no error is revealed integrity and access is granted. The MAC, for example, can be generated by hashing data of the heartbeat and ciphering it with the key.

The effort of safety and security measure differs. Safe addresses are for example 3 byte [NOV07], a CRC typically is 2 byte and a MAC is 4 to 16 byte long. Generating a CRC on an embedded device takes some tens to hundreds of microseconds, whereas calculating a MAC requires tens of milliseconds. On producer side time to copy safe address into message and on consumer side time to check safe addresses are microscopic and not considered. In short, safety and security measures differ in terms of performance and bandwidth overhead.

Let's assume a safety critical environment, a hospital, and a safety critical service: a fire alarm system. Heartbeats have to be sent between a fire detector (producer) and a fire damper (consumer). Timing requirements of such a service are relaxed: reaction time is somewhere in the order of minutes until a fire damper has to be triggered. Consequently, heartbeats are sent every tens of seconds and so some tens of milliseconds to generate and check the MAC are not critical. Albeit a safety critical service, a security related measure is applied and hence intentional attacks are considered.

In case of an emergency push button service to stop the revolving door at the entrance, requirements on the reaction time are far stricter. The door has to stop within hundreds of milliseconds in order not to hurt someone having fallen down. Heartbeats have to be sent every tens of milliseconds and therefore safety measure is chosen. In case of an access control system to a vault the situation is different. Heartbeats are sent between an actuator to open the door and the input screen. If we assume that the door of the vault can be opened manually from the inside – low risk level to people being inside the vault –, strong authentication (generating a MAC) has priority to avoid unauthorized access to the actuator.

8. Safety-security Requirements

In the last two chapters the common approach was presented and discussed regarding the whole system, the building automation and control system (BACS). According to [IEC12] a system is "an integrated composite that consists of one or more of the [lifecycle] processes, hardware, software, facilities and people, that provides a capability to satisfy a stated need or objective."

As mentioned in chapter 6, it has to be distinguished between the system and (multiple) entity safety-security lifecycle models. Activities in Fig. 6-1 that include the word 'overall' meaning 'system wide' are considering the system during execution whilst the other activities are to be performed for every entity in the system. It has to be emphasized that the different tasks of an activity are identical in every entity lifecycle. That is why there is only one safety-security lifecycle model. However, the results during the non-overall activities differ, e.g. the hardware architecture of a node and a gateway are different. Put another way, the entity lifecycle models are instantiated multiple times and are input to the system lifecycle model as shown in Fig. 8-1.

8.1 Scope of Use Case

In the chapter the pre-design process of the safety-security lifecycle model of a subsystem or entity, the node, is outlined. The node is taken as example to present the lifecycle model because it may be safety *and* security critical. The same is valid for a management device. A gateway, for example, is not safety critical because it just tunnels safety related messages and does not process them at all. However, if the gateway also interprets the payload, i.e. changes the format of a data value in the payload field of the message, it is safety critical because it processes the safety related message. For instance, that is the case when data points from LonWorks are mapped to BACnet. Moreover, a node by contrast to a management device is an embedded device. Thus, standard IT security measures such as TLS [RFC22] using asymmetric cryptography cannot be applied efficiently due to the enormous computational and message overhead. As mentioned in [NOV05, p. 21], asymmetric cryptographic operation on a smartcard takes up to 50% longer than symmetric cryptographic ones. In addition, the key size of an asymmetric cipher is 64 byte [RSA78] whereas the one of a symmetric cipher is 8 byte long [NIS46-2]. Embedded devices such as a node are low power entities equipped with very limited memory resources. To identify commonalities between safety and security in order to reduce effort, is therefore of greatest importance on node side.

The following use case, i.e. development of a safe-secure node and integration into the BACS, is based on knowledge gained from two EU funded projects: REMPLI (Real-time Energy Management via Power lines and Internet) [NOV05] and SafetyLon [NOV07, HER08].

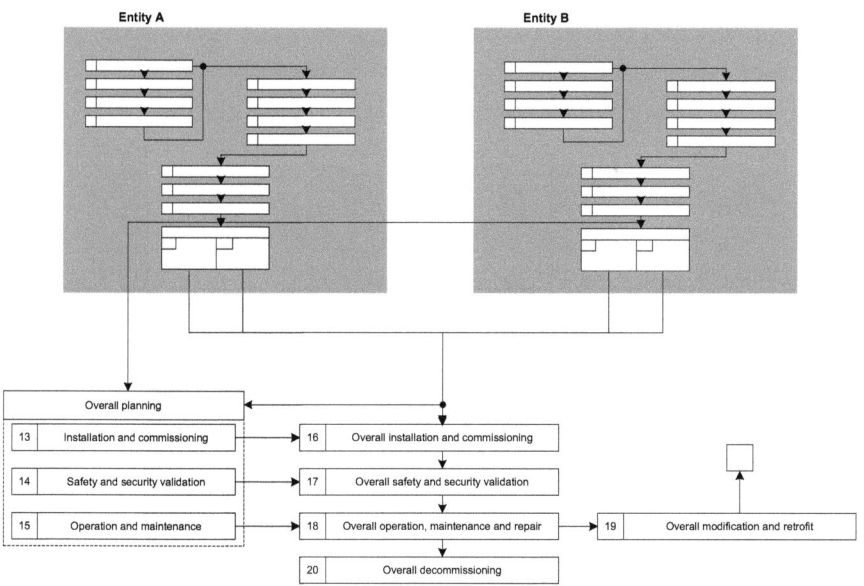

Fig. 8-1 Relationship between entity and system lifecycle model

The REMPLI project deals with the design and implementation of a communication infrastructure for distributed data acquisition and remote control operations, referred to as SCADA (supervisory control and data acquisition) tasks, using the power grid as communication medium. The intention of such an infrastructure is to allow remote meter reading and to gain more information on the energy consumption of end users. Security critical high level services such as energy billing can be built upon the REMPLI system.

The goal of the SafetyLon project is to enhance LonWorks [EN149], both the protocol as well as the nodes, with additional features to meet the safety requirements of safety integrity level 3 (SIL 3) [IEC61]. Additionally, management tools are adapted to the safety needs. SafetyLon is the first BACS that meets safety requirements, and is prepared to be used for safety critical application like fire alarm systems.

In detail, the use case focuses on pointing out dependencies between safety and security regarding technical issues, e.g. hardware and software architecture, functional safety-security measures, or testing methods. Less attention is paid to safety-security management or infrastructure, i.e. organizational processes. Nevertheless, they are absolutely important for succeeding in developing and using a safe-secure BACS.

8.2 Definition of the Concept

The intention of a BACS developed and used according to the requirements of the safety-security lifecycle is to provide safe-secure communication among nodes to send process data to actuators or controllers as well as to enable transport service from nodes to a management device. Problems to be tackled are the safe communication among nodes and to the management device; additionally, secure communication among nodes and to the gateway in the field level. Ensuring secure communication between gateway and management device is accomplished by standard security measures

The goal of the use case is to develop a safe-secure node that is integrated into a standard field level network, i.e. the fieldbus. Reaction time of the node, i.e. time between getting an input and sending a message has to be about 300 ms. The physical medium of the network is TP/FT-10 channel [EN149-2] with a bandwidth of 78,1 kbit/s. The transport protocol is called LonTalk [EN149-1] that provides the routing service. The hardware used to access the network is either the Shortstack Microserver [ECH02] or the LC3020 [LOY05]. They differ in computational power and memory resources as presented in subchapter 3.3.

Each safe-secure node is able to process safe-secure and non-safe-secure messages. Furthermore, safe-secure nodes and standard nodes are connected to the same network. The standard node must be enhanced with hardware and software functions so that it receives input from sensors and sends output to actuators safely. It provides safety-security functions to allow safe-secure message exchange with the management device and with other nodes.

Functionality to meet safety-security requirements is encapsulated in a safe-secure firmware. Software programmed to execute a task by using the firmware of a safe-secure node is called application software. Firmware is logically located above layer 7 of the ISO/OSI reference model [ISO74]. The reasons are the following: In the safety world a requirement is to prove that the residual failure probability is below a maximum level. To avoid investigation of the standard protocol regarding failure probability, it is treated as 'black channel'. I.e., it is assumed that is does not contribute to failure probability reduction. Therefore, only the safety software must be considered when calculating the residual failure probability [REI01, p. 32]. Second, locating security above layer 7 makes end-to-end security possible. Desired in most security applications [REY05] where the standard protocol stack should remain unchanged. Finally, regarding standard LonWorks nodes, integration of safety-security functions into the different layers of the OSI reference model is not possible because they are fully implemented in hardware and firmware without the change of alteration. Additionally, full compliance with the LonTalk standard is given [SCH03].

Due to the enormous amount of nodes, it must be possible to setup and manage the safe-secure system remotely via a management device. Consequently, standard management tools must be enhanced with a plug-in and safe-secure nodes have to support the safe-secure network management commands. Network installation is therefore divided into two steps: first, the standard procedure is applied to establish the logical communication paths (the so called binding). After that a safe-secure procedure is executed, the so called safe-secure-binding.

The system shall comply with requirements of safety integrity level 3 (SIL 3) and evaluation assurance level 3 (EAL 3). To explain the reason for a target SIL 3, refer to the risk graph in Fig. 6-3 taken from IEC 61508. Severity of hazards resulting from BAC systems are in between insignificant C_1 and very significant C_3, but not disastrous C_4, i.e. death of thousands of people. Significant hazards resulting from bit fault occur often F_3 and cannot be avoided P_2, very significant faults leading to a hardware failures occur likely F_2 and also cannot be avoided P_2. However, such a failure do not occur very often F_4, since BAC systems are typically not operating in EMC critical environments compared to industrial automation systems. Failures in general do not W_1 or sometime occur W_2, especially during management activities. In short, a SIL 3 BACS takes into account injury of humans and death of a human.

According to IEC15-3, EAL 3 permits maximum assurance from positive security engineering at the design stage. EAL 3 is referred to as methodically tested and checked and provides a moderate level of confidence in the correct operation of security functions [HER03, p. 184]. The level ensures a rather high testing coverage, similar to the one required by SIL 3. It is an adequate level especially regarding the field level network that is susceptible to denial-of-service attacks, but not to viruses, worms or faulty updates.

Target safety integrity and evaluation assurance level are determined at the beginning and action are taken to meet requirements of the corresponding levels. Such an approach is chosen because the BACS shall cover applications like fire alarm, access control, intrusion detection, or emergency lighting. In that field of application the defined target SIL is mandatory and target EAL desired.

8.3 Safety Dependent Activities

The scope of the safety hazard and risk analysis is the node connected to the fieldbus. On the one hand, hazards resulting from failures on the network must be investigated that are influencing node safety. It is not intended to ensure network safety because the network is part of the black channel and not included into safety considerations. On the other hand, the node itself has to be examined regarding failures. Moreover, the risk caused by the failures must be assessed and countermeasures according to the chosen SIL must be specified.

Table 8-1 lists typical network faults. The faults can be categorized in three different groups: faults directly corresponding to human mistakes (8, 9), faults not directly relating to human mistakes (1-7), and faults either directly or indirectly referring to human mistakes (10). The cause of such a grouping is to point out that human mistakes must be considered during investigation of (network) faults. In [SCH00, pp. 255] it is called the 'human factor' saying that humans are the weakest link.

Table 8-1 Typical network faults [REI01, p. 32]

1. Crosstalk	6. Aging
2. Broken cable	7. Temperature
3. EMC failure	8. Human failure
4. Stochastic failure	9. Wiring failure
5. Stuck at failure	10. Transmission of non-authorized messages

The next step is to identify the network failures resulting from faults listed in Table 8-1. Network failures can be separated into stochastic, i.e. hardware failures, and systematic failures as mentioned in subchapter 4.1. Such failures lead to hazards and must be countered by adequate countermeasures as presented in Table 8-2.

Risk analysis can be performed by quantifying or qualifying the risk. As already mentioned in subchapter 6.1, stochastic or hardware failures can be quantified, others only qualified by specifying discrete levels such as 'low', 'medium', or 'high'. For example, risk of a 'bits being destroyed' can be calculated the following. According to [PHO97], the probability of a bit being destroyed on shielded twisted pair cables is $p = 10^{-5}$. It is assumed that $v = 10$ safety related messages are sent every second. The rate of transmission errors U is [REI01, p. 40]:

$$U_1 = p*v = 10^{-4}/s$$

In other words, every 10000 seconds a single transmission error occurs and the risk of being a single bit destroyed per seconds is 10^{-4}. The probability that two bits are destroyed is $10^{-9}/s$, assuming that probabilities are independent and therefore p^2 is inserted into the aforementioned formula. As a result, a safety integrity requirement is that a CRC must be chosen so that the residual failure probability of a mes-

Safety-security Requirements

sage is at least below 10^{-7}/hour (Table 4-1). Additionally, data duplication has to be used, i.e. definition of a safe message format.

Table 8-2 Safety requirement specification (network failures)

Failure	Hazard	Safety requirement
Single bit destroyed	A new message can be produced which can cause malfunctions.	Check with a CRC
Lots of bits destroyed	A new message can be produced which can cause malfunctions.	Duplication of message and comparison of both messages
Malfunction of the network (e.g. broken wire), entity	A safety related message cannot reach the consumer.	Send messages periodically (heartbeat) and use a watchdog
Malfunction of entity (of a producer)	A safety related message cannot reach the consumer.	Send messages periodically (heartbeat) and use a watchdog
Malfunction of the network access unit	A message is received, but these messages do not correspond to actual values.	Use of a watchdog, use of a timestamp
Loss of a message	A safety related message cannot reach the consumer.	Send messages periodically (heartbeat) and use a watchdog
Insertion of a message	An old message, which has been stored for a certain time reappears, or the message is doubled, or another entity adds a new message.	Use of safe source addresses
Repetition of a message	An old message, which has been stored for a certain time reappears, or a message is doubled by the producer or a network entity.	Use of a timestamp
Wrong sequence of messages	The sequence of messages differs from the actual one.	Use of a timestamp
Delay of a message	The message may be delayed due to a network entity. The value is not valid any more.	Use of a timestamp
Non-safety related message	A non-safety related message looks like a safety related message. Or, a non safety related message prevents a safety related message from being sent.	Use of a specific header, use of a safe source address, use of a timestamp, use of a watchdog

The target SIL does not only affect the safety integrity of safety functions, but also the hardware architecture of a node. As shown in Table 4-2, there is the possibility to either increase the hardware fault tolerance or the safe failure fraction (SFF) to achieve a target SIL. With regard to SIL 3 three ways are possible: Implement safety functions so that more than 99% failures do not result in a critical situation, or use a dual channel architecture (see Fig. 6-7), i.e. introduce hardware redundancy and guarantee that 90-99% of all failures do not cause a critical situation, or use a three channel structure and care for a safe failure fraction of 60-90%.

Using no hardware redundancy requires very resource and time consuming measures such as very sophisticated online self tests to grant a SFF of greater 99%. For example, self tests have to be implemented to test the volatile memory of the microcontroller that executes the safety functions. A memory test with a high diagnostic coverage (DC) is the galloping pattern test. It test effort is equal to $2*(2^N+2n^2)$ [WRA07, p. 211] where N is the number of address bits and n the number of memory cells in bits. Such tests cannot be executed on standard LonWorks network access units (NAU).

As a consequence, a 1oo2 structure is selected. In general, there are two possible solutions to design such a structure: the NAU is considered to be the first channel and an additional safety chip is the second channel. However, the problem is that the Neuron Chip is not powerful enough regarding computational power and memory resources. Hence, just the LC3020 can be used, but hardware interfaces have to be redesigned to meet safety requirements. The second and better solution is to use both NAUs only to access the network. The node is designed so that it consists of two additional safety chips.

Also failures on node side must be investigated. That is, a hazard analysis and risk analysis has also to be performed to identify failures on the node itself (Table 8-3). In [IEC61-2] a detailed list is provided that gives information on the various failures in the components of a microcontroller that must be taken into consideration. Such a hazard analysis can be carried out by means of a failure mode and effects analysis (FMEA) – refer to subchapter 6.1.

In literature such as [GIE95] or [LIG02] failure rates for standard hardware components are listed. Failure rates are available for resistors, diodes, transistors or capacitors and the like, and are quantified in FIT (failure in time) which equals a risk of

10^{-9}/hour. They are used to perform the risk analysis. For example, a risk resulting from the input device is a combination of failures rates of different components finally leading to a quantified risk value for the complete circuit. The same is true for the CPU, or static and volatile memory. See [BOE04, pp. 107; BOE07, pp. 260; WRA07, pp. 73] for examples how to calculate failures rates of circuits. Yet again, safety integrity requirements are derived from the risk analysis. E.g., test pulses must be sent every 2 seconds to ensure that residual failure probability is below the target level, or diagnostic coverage of RAM test must be about 90%.

Table 8-3 Safety requirement specification (hardware node failures)

Hardware component	Failure	Effect	Safety requirement
Controller	Malfunction	Wrong operation of device	Use of a 1oo2 structure with watchdog and cross-checking; Use of cyclic communication via serial interface between both channels; use of CPU test at startup and during operation
Memory	Wrong values stored	Wrong operation of device	Use of memory test at startup and during operation
Input device	Stuck at failure or shortcut failure between different channels	Wrong operation of device	Use of test pulses; use of test pattern with different test pulses
Output device to NAU	Stochastic and systematic failures during data transfer	Wrong operation of device	Check of message by independent channels and comparison of check-results
Output device to actuator	Failure of output switch	Unable to switch off	Use of test pulses

8.4 Security Dependent Activities

Security activities start with an investigation of the security environment. First of all, it has to be clarified where entities in the field level network are placed. In [SCH02] it is distinguished between a controlled network where the entities are under control of the user who is the owner, and an uncontrolled network where the entities are under control of a user who is not the owner and therefore considered to be an adversary. Definitely, the nodes in the use case are located in an uncontrolled and hostile environment.

The physical environment of the node consist of 2 safety chips and a network access unit (NAU); moreover, of sensors and actuators connected to a node. However, the boundaries of the Target of Evaluation (TOE), i.e. the part that is subject to node security considerations, are the hardware interfaces to the sensors and actuators, and the interface to the NAU. Put another way, communication lines to actuators and sensors, and to the NAU are not included into security investigation.

The next step is identification of the assets. That is, information or resources requiring protection are identified and valued afterwards. As mentioned in subchapter 6.1, assets are categorized into three groups. Two of them are under investigation in the following: operational data that the TOE stores, and TOE hardware, software and firmware. Additionally, the are valued by specifying four levels 'low', 'medium', 'high' and 'highest' as shown in Table 8-4.

Without proper process data the BACS is not working. Services to be provided by the system simply rely on the data. It is the core of the BACS informational resources [GOR00, p. 74]. As a consequence, they are assigned the value 'high'.

Diagnostic information and security audit and fail safe data are separated although the second one can be seen as part of the first one. Diagnostic information compromise information on the number of missing input and output test pulses, or the number of failures during communication between the safety chips or safety chip and NAU. Such data is interesting to evaluate quality in general and therefore is ranked 'low'. Security audit and fail safe data summarizes information on security and safety critical events such as the number of unauthorized accesses to sensor data, or the specification of a hardware failure detected during execution of an on-line memory test. Such information is valued with 'medium' since it gives advice of attacks or defects.

Network management data, e.g. safe-secure binding data, is ranked 'medium'. It is important for setting up a system, but it need not to be available immediately and to be protected from disclosure.

TOE hardware, software, firmware must operate correctly to ensure the proper operation of safe and secure applications. A higher number of malfunction of node hardware or the scheduler decreases availability of functionality. Hence, the two assets are ranked 'high'. Disclosure of the cryptographic keys results in breaching the security of the *whole* system and is ranked 'highest'.

Aforementioned hardware boundaries and security objectives to be specified next are based upon the following assumptions.

- The communication between a node and a sensor or actuator is not susceptible to security attacks. Connection to sensors or actuators is realized by a dedicated line that is not accessible from the outside.

- The interface to NAU and between the safety chips is realized by a serial interface and not accessible from the outside.

- Cryptographic measures will be resistant to cryptanalytic attacks [HER03, p. 75].

- Keys used in cryptographic measures are located within controlled access components that prevent unauthorized physical access. Communication line to such components is not accessible from the outside.

- Hardware components of the node like a smartcard cannot be replaced.

- A single organization is responsible for installing, configuring, maintaining and controlling the network [SCH03].

Table 8-4 Assets, value of assets, risk of threats and resulting risk level

Operational data of the TOE	Value	Threat risk	Risk level
Input (sensor) data	high	highest	highest
Output (actuator) data	high	highest	highest
Diagnostic information	low	medium	medium
Security audit and fail safe data	medium	high	high
Network management data	medium	medium	medium
TOE hardware, software, firmware			
Safety chips	high	low	medium
Software functions scheduler	high	medium	high
Cryptographic keys	highest	highest	highest

After determination of assets and assumptions threats to the assets are identified and risk associated with the threats is assessed. Generally, threats can be classified into three groups: *interception, sabotage, manipulation* [GOR00, p. 78]. Interception denotes an unauthorized access to information violating node data confidentiality. Sabotage means prevention or denial of node functionality as well as destruction of node resources and therefore is threatening integrity and availability. Manipulation endangers confidentiality, integrity and availability, and can be separated into modification, deletion, insertion and replay.

Input and output data has to be protected against attacks relating to the integrity, availability and authenticity of data. Since an actuator is reacting according to the sensor data, integrity and authenticity must be granted. Furthermore, to ensure a high availability of the node, such data must be on-hand when needed. However, confidentiality is not of importance. Why should the command 'stop the machine' after pressing an emergency button be protected against disclosure? Attackers do not get information to break security. Consequently, input and output data must be secured against sabotage and manipulation.

Diagnostic information, security and fail safe data, and network management data are relevant to manage and maintain the system, and to react to safety-security critical events on node side. Hence, integrity and authenticity must be ensured since diagnostic information, and security and fail safe data are the basis to respond in case of obvious malfunctions. Network management data, in turn, is the basis to setup and maintain the system. Availability and confidentiality are not taken into account because first if node data is not available for some time, a malfunction in general must be assumed. Second, revealing for example security audit data does not help to manipulate, but maybe to evaluate the quality of the system. As a consequence, threats resulting from sabotage and manipulation have to be considered.

The safety-security related node hardware, i.e. the safety chips, and the part of the firmware that schedules the functions have to be guarded against sabotage, in particular the safety chips, and manipulation, not against replay, but insertion, deletion and modification. Integrity of hardware and software is a prerequisite so that safety-security functionality can be provided according to expectation.

Cryptographic keys are required to communicate in a secure way. Since symmetric keys are preferred in field level networks (see subchapter 6.3), they must be kept secret on the node and transferred securely to the right node. Additionally, they must be on hand when a message should be secured. As a result, confidentiality, integrity, availability, and authenticity have to be ensured and functions are required to counter interception, sabotage and manipulation.

Whereas it is a common practice to use a quantitative approach for risk assessment – see [BOE04, pp. 15] for various examples –, security often uses a qualitative approach. Quantitative approaches in the security domain do not use failure probabilities, but solely assesses risk in terms of money. A criterion is the annual loss expectancy (ALE) [SCH00, pp. 301]. The basic idea is to take all the threats, estimate the expected loss per incident and amount of incidents per annum.

To assess the risk, the risk matrix presented in Table 6-1 is applied. At first, threats to the assets have to be valued, i.e. the threat likelihood must be specified (Table 8-4). Since input and output data are processed and sent on a regular basis, risk of threat is 'high'. Diagnostic information gives information on the quality of the node and is not directly corresponding to security critical events. Threats are not very likely and the risk is determined to be 'medium'. On the contrary, security audit and fail safe data relates to safety-security critical events. They may give the attacker a feedback. That is, he can verify if his attack was recognized. Risk level of the threat is 'high'. Network management data is processed and sent at a defined time (installation of the node). Afterwards its use is absolutely unpredictable for an attacker, though. That is the reason why the risk of threat is 'medium'.

Table 8-5 Security requirements related to TOE

Security objective	Security requirements	Security functional family
Authorization	Use of an access control function	FDP_ACF
Integrity, Authenticity	Use of message authentication code (MAC)	FIA_UAU, FDP_DAU
Confidentiality	Use of a symmetric cipher	FDP_ITT, FDP_UCT, FPT_ITC, FPT_ITT
Availability	Use of fault tolerance mechanism	FRU_FLT

Threat risk to safety chips is low because the node itself is mostly not or hardly physical accessible. Software functions scheduler is running permanently and is therefore on the one hand easy to attack. On the other hand it can only be accessed indirectly since it does not provide functionality to the outside. Hence, threat risk is 'medium'. Cryptographic keys are used frequently and are exchanged at installation at a defined time. The risk of threat is ranked 'highest'.

Taking the value of assets and the risk of threat levels as input to the risk matrix in Table 6-1, output as shown in Table 8-4 is received. Next security objectives must be determined. Most of them were already mentioned during discussion of the threats: confidentiality, integrity, availability and authenticity. A further security objective is authorization meaning that all assets should only be accessed and processed by the ones that are allowed to.

Security requirements are derived from the security objectives in the next step. Requirement specification also accounts for the organizational security policy (OSP). It specifies rules, procedures and guidelines for the different lifecycle activities. In the use case the OSP consists of a single rule: 'Topics related to safety must be in accordance with IEC 61508'. Security requirements can be divided into functional and assurance ones (see subchapter 4.2). Since the evaluation assurance level was already fixed (EAL 3), in the following only security functional requirements are dealt with.

Table 8-6 Security requirements related to operational environment

Reason	Security requirements	Security functional class
Security operations (MAC, cipher)	Use of cryptographic keys	FCS
Non-disclosure of keys	Smartcard support	-
Update keys simultaneously	Use of timestamps	FPT_STM
Reaction to attacks	Security audit	FAU
Integrity of software functions scheduler	Use of online self tests	FPT_TST

Table 8-5 shows security requirements directly relating to the security objectives. And the dedicated security functional family in [IEC15-2] is listed that gives the detailed requirements. Additionally, Table 8-6 presents security requirements that are specified in order to support requirements mentioned in Table 8-5. For example, symmetric ciphers are used to grant confidentiality of data. Such ciphers use cryptographic keys to cipher the data. The keys, in turn, must not be disclosed since symmetric ciphers with private keys are applied. In the end, keys are subject to attacks and have to be updated.

8.5 Safety and Security Integration

As a result from the safety dependent activities a safety requirement specification is available. A security requirement specification, in Fig. 6-5 referred to as protection profile, is the output of the security dependent activities. The next step is to perform the conflict resolution and measure assessment to receive a conflict free set of safety-security requirements that are influencing hardware, software and lifecycle process requirements as shown in Fig. 8-2.

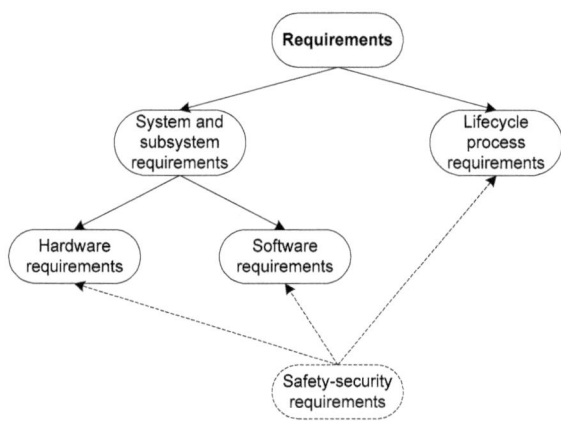

Fig. 8-2 Influence of safety-security requirements on different types of requirements

In the following only such safety and security requirements are examined that have an impact on hardware and software requirements of the node. Others are out of the scope of the use case. However, they are of great importance and lots of commonalities can be found. Examples are: requirements on the configuration management; requirements on the type of testing, requirements on the use of methods to avoid design faults or requirements on documentation mentioned in [IEC15-3] and [IEC61-2, IEC61-3].

Before starting with conflict resolution, a conflict resolution policy has to be specified. In the use case the policy consists of two rules:

1. Prefer safety requirements to security requirements if security reduces safety.
2. Otherwise, use security requirement in order to consider also intentional attacks.

According to Fig. 7-4, the first step of the conflict resolution approach is to group the requirements into three categories: first, detective requirements such as 'Use of a timestamp', or 'Use of a CRC/MAC to detect integrity faults. Such requirements lead to functions that detect faults or incidents; second, preventive requirements like 'Use of symmetric ciphers', or 'Use of an access control to prevent from unauthorized access to resources'. The type of requirements results in function aiming at avoiding failures or incidents; third, corrective requirements that specify actions to be taken after a failure or incident has occurred. As mentioned in subchapter 7.2.1, requirements of the type are likely to be conflicting.

Table 8-7 shows four corrective safety and security requirements, respectively. They are specified because of a fault or incident being detected by a detective function. The first fault leads to a 'hardware failure'. For instance, the online volatile memory test revealed a fault in a sector of the RAM of the first safety chip. From the safety point of view it is required that the safety chip switches to fail safe state immediately. Since both chips absolutely must agree on everything that should be executed (two channel architecture), fail safe state of one results in fail safe state of the complete node. Security requirement says that the first chip has to go to fail secure state and the second one takes over. The conflict is solved by taking the safety and discarding the security requirement. In the case security reduces safety – rule one of the conflict resolution approach.

The second fault leading to an 'integrity failure' results in similar safety and security requirements. Such a failure is detected due to CRC or MAC mismatches. Safety requirement is part of the security requirement. As security does not reduce safety, the security requirement is chosen – rule two of the conflict resolution approach. Failure 3 and incident 4 have no impact on security and safety, respectively. Consequently, the safety requirement as a reaction to 'Message lost' and the security requirement to 'Disclosure of key' is determined to be a final safety-security requirement.

Table 8-7 Corrective safety and security requirements

Failure/incident	Safety requirement	Security requirement
1. Hardware failure	Fail-safe state of node	Fail-secure state of safety chip
2. Integrity failure	Discard message	Discard message; after five successive incidents send message to network management device to signal attack.
3. Message lost	Fail-safe state of consumer	none
4. Disclosure of key	none	Stop communication until new key available

At this stage a few commonalities between safety and security can be identified. Beside similar tools (e.g. methods to identify risk) and approaches for analysis, some safety and security requirements are identical. If safety and security measures are used jointly and not installed in parallel, a potential for high synergies can be acquired. In the following an example of measure assessment as outlined in subchapter 7.2.2 is given.

In a safety related system a source addressing model is used to guarantee message exchange between safe nodes only and to avoid message insertion of non-safety related messages (see Table 8-2). Therefore each *producer* is assigned an additional unique address, a so called *safe address*. The receiving consumer checks this safe address against its access list and only allows reception of messages in the list. The safety integrity is given by a CRC checking and by the transfer of a safe address within the safe message which can only be generated by safe nodes.

Access control to network management data is realized by specifying a protocol different from the one used to exchange process data. Therefore, each *node* gets a safe address. Additionally, the exchange is based on a request/respond model where only the network management device sends a request to a node with a defined safe address and just a node sends a response. Hence, it is guaranteed that only a network management device can read or write management data.

In a secure system similar measures are used. An access control is also based on the node address, but instead of the CRC a cryptographic message authentication code (MAC) is used that cannot be recalculated without the knowledge of the appropriate key. According to the node address and in case of a proven authenticity of the message, data can be read or written.

A matching of the requirements and measures can lead to synergies in the design of a safe-secure system. In the example the CRC is replaced by the MAC which allows removing the safe address. Access control is now managed by standard network addresses and the requirement to identify producers belonging to the consumer is realized by a particular key only available to the producer and consumer. Moreover, each node shares a unique key with the network management device. Assuming a 1 byte CRC and a safe address of 3 byte [NOV07], overhead in every message part is 4 byte. Since data is duplicated to ensure a minimum of residual failure probability (see Table 8-2), the overhead of each message is 8 byte. On the contrary, a 3-DES [NIS46-3] MAC as mentioned in [NOV05, pp. 29] is also 8 byte long. That is, message length does not increase, but message is guarded against intentional attacks also. And implementation of a further protocol is not required any longer since every node and the network management device protect their messages with a unique key.

In general, security measures will replace safety measures since measures designed for safety do not withstand intentional attacks. E.g., a CRC protects the integrity of a message, but can be recalculated online. Hence stochastic faults are discovered, but an attacker is not impeded to manipulate the targeted information (asset) as well as the CRC. Important factors to be considered when replacing safety measures are shown in Fig. 7-7.

Table 8-8 Performance of security functions [TRE05]

Description	Time [ms]
Cipher message using 3-DES in outer CBC mode	58
Decipher message using 3-DES in outer CBC mode	55
Authenticate message with 8-byte MAC using 3-DES in outer CBC mode	53
Verify 8-byte MAC using 3-DES in outer CBC mode	47

First, safety integrity must not be jeopardized, i.e. the residual failure probability value has to be similar to the one before replacement of safety measures. In other words, a MAC must be selected that grants the same level of integrity than the non-secure CRC does. A possible way to solve the problem is introduced in [KRA94]: use of cryptographic CRCs. They are based on the same operations as a standard CRC is based on, but are combined with a one-time pad (i.e. a random irreducible polynomial) or a secure stream cipher. The advantage of such a cryptographic CRC is that mathematical methods used to calculate the residual failure probability of a standard CRC – a must in the safety world – can also be applied to the cryptographic CRC. In contrast, it is a challenging task to produce a large number 'real' random polynomials [STA03, pp. 43].

Second, according to the evaluation assurance level (EAL) a minimum strength of function is specified and has to be proven. Put another way, the MAC has to be chosen in a way so that it cannot be defeated. It must adhere to the three properties mentioned in subchapter 1.3.

Third, software and hardware environment has to be considered. Using a smartcard with a symmetric cipher algorithm being implemented in hardware, results in less computational time than calculating the same algorithm in software. Furthermore, memory resources of embedded devices are low compared to PCs. Replacing the safe address of 3 byte to be stored in an access list as identification of a producer by a 8 byte key, increases memory consumption. On the other hand, since the implementation of a network management protocol is not required, some memory space is saved. Whereas memory space required for the network management protocol is a constant value, memory consumption of keys depends and raises with the number of producers a message is received from. Since it is assumed that a safe-secure node does not receive messages of more than 20-40 different producers, security measure is applied. The assumption is based on the requirement stated in Table 8-2: Heartbeats must be sent on a regular basis (e.g. every hundred milliseconds or every 5 seconds) by a producer and processed by the consumer to reset the watchdog. Due to the low bandwidth, congestion on the network is inevitable and functionality is reduced when 60 producers send heartbeats to a single node. Bandwidth overhead, however, does not change whether the safety or the security measure is used.

Table 8-9 Safety-security requirements

Hazard, threat	Safety-security requirement
Loss of a message	Send heartbeats and use a watchdog
Insertion of a message	Use of a MAC and timestamp, store information of last message received
Replay of a message	Timestamp, store information of last message received
Wrong sequence of messages	Timestamp, store information of last message received
Delay of message	Timestamp
Modification of data	Use of a MAC
Disclosure of data	Data encryption
Unauthorized access to data	Access control
Availability of data	Data duplication (hardware architecture)
Software function scheduler modification	Software monitoring
Failure in volatile, non-volatile memory, and CPU	Online self tests
Failure in input, output device	Test pulses, test pattern

Finally, performance of measures and the impact on field of application are examined. Referring to Table 8-8, generating and verifying a 8 byte CBC-MAC [NIS11] on a smartcard takes about 50 ms of time whereas the process of calculating a CRC like the ones mentioned in [KOO04] lasts about 300-500 μs [PRE06, pp. 90]. Consequently, ensuring integrity with a MAC excludes applications like emergency push button since an overall reaction time, i.e. time from pressing the button on Node A and stopping a machine connected to Node B, of less than 150 ms is required [REI01, p. 27]. A requirement specified in the concept of the uses case is to have a node reaction time of 300 ms – so a MAC is the preferred choice.

Table 8-9 presents the final detective and preventive safety-security requirements. A lot of synergies are identified that reduce implementation and computational effort:

- Safe address of node used as node identification to perform a security access control

- Timestamps to detect network failures and carry out key updates synchronously
- MAC to verify integrity and authenticity of messages or data on a node
- Hardware tests like RAM tests support integrity of software function scheduler.
- The 1oo2 channel architecture increases data availability.

Moreover, corrective requirements are listed in Table 8-7. Together with the implementation requirements specified during measure assessment (e.g. quality of the MAC) they are the base for hardware and software realization.

9. Software Realization

The safety-security requirements are the basis of hardware and software realization as shown in Fig. 6-6. They are influencing the software requirements and the hardware architecture. The last mentioned is dealt with at the beginning of the chapter. An overview of the architecture of the node is presented, not a close look to the details (e.g. hardware schematics of a safe input) is made. Put succinctly, hardware is discussed with the level of detail required to understand the software design.

The chapter focuses on the software design, the development and testing, and the operation of the node software. A high level view of the activities of lifecycle micro-processes is presented in the following, not discussing software modules in detail neither presenting implementation aspects such as source code listings. The software lifecycle model is the V-model [BRO93] because it is the basis of the software safety lifecycle mentioned in [IEC61-3]. Additional activities are integrated taken from an approach to software security (subchapter 5.2.4) – the idea of engineering software in a way so that it also works correctly under malicious attacks [MCG06, p. 3].

9.1 Hardware Architecture

The hardware architecture as shown in Fig. 9-1 consists of two microcontrollers, Saf-sec Chip 1 and Saf-sec Chip 2. They are implemented to satisfy the requirement 'Use of a 1oo2 structure' (a two channel structure) listed in Table 8-3. The first channel is Saf-sec Chip 1 and the second Saf-sec Chip 2.

In a 1oo2 structure always both channels have to agree to perform an operation like setting a safe output or reading an input. For that reason both saf-sec chips are connected to the safety related input/output unit. The unit consists of circuits designed in such a way that they also can be tested by means of test pulses with test pattern. More information on test circuits can be found in [WRA07, pp. 79].

Smartcards equipped with a microcontroller are used as a security token to store cryptographic keys and protect them from disclosure. Additionally, network management data is stored in the EEPROM of the smartcard. As the channels have to carry out the same task on their own and data availability ought to be increased, each safe-secure node consists of two smartcards. In the architecture presented in Fig. 9-1 a further intention of the integration of the smartcard is to support node security. On the contrary to two other approaches mentioned in [PAL03] where the smartcard is the interface to the network or the interface to the input/output unit, in the architecture the smartcard cares for operations with symmetric keys such as ciphering or authenticating a message.

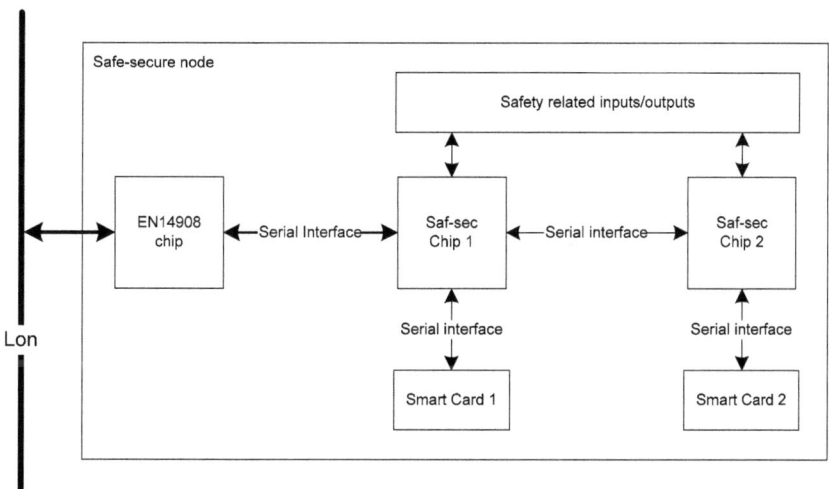

Fig. 9-1 Safe-secure node hardware architecture

Smartcards are the preferred choice because they are small, well standardized in ISO 7816 [ISO78], tamper-proof, i.e. physically protected and not accessible in an unauthorized manner, and consume very little power [SCH03]. It has to be mentioned though that they are not invulnerable against any kind of attack [SCH00, pp. 222]. The drawback compared to a simple secure EEPROM is the additional programming effort. Programs on the smartcard must be developed to handle the keys used for security operations and other data, and to perform the security operations.

Network access is realized by a single dedicated network access unit (NAU), the EN 14908 chip: Shortstack Microserver or LC3020. Such architecture corresponds to the one illustrated in Fig. 6-8(c). It is the same architecture used for nodes in SafetyBUS p as outlined in subchapter 3.4. It was selected because seen from the network side a safe-secure node behaves like a standard node. It has a single unique network ID, sends and receives messages, is accessible and configurable via standard network management tools. Thus, installation and maintenance of the BACS can be accomplished in a convenient way. As an one-to-one relationship between NAU and Safe-sec Chip 1 is specified, synchronization of sending to and receiving messages from the EN 14908 chip is easy to manage via a serial interface. Last but not least, less hardware compared to other architectures shown in Fig. 6-8 results in fewer costs – very important when thinking of systems with thousands of nodes.

9.2 Design

The firmware is organized in a three layered architecture and located above ISO/OSI layer 7 – equal to the approach chosen in PROFIsafe (refer to subchapter 3.4) – as shown in Fig. 9-2. Since only Saf-sec Chip 1 is connected to the EN 14908 chip, the lower layer differs between the chips. Shortstack API and Saf-sec Chip Orion Stack API, respectively, are third-party ISO/OSI layer 7 software located below the first layer of the firmware. They care for the transmission of data from and to the chosen EN 14908 chip. Their software is not part of safety and security considerations. They are already part of the 'black channel' and hence not outlined in the following.

On top of the firmware is the *application layer interface*. It offers the application programmer functions that are used to realize safe-secure application software. Typical functions are sending and receiving functions, writing to and reading from the smartcard, receiving value from the safety related input or setting the safety related output, or write and read access to the sensor and actuator data stored in a table being part of the safe-secure software. The application layer interface provides a convenient way of programming safety-security applications without taking care of safety-security functions encapsulated in the safety-security layer.

A part of the first safety-security firmware layer is called *network access layer interface*. It is an abstraction layer that makes access to the LON possible regardless of the underlying third-party software, the Shortstack API with the Shortstack Microserver or the Saf-sec Chip Orion Stack API with the LC3020. Functions of the network access layer are declared in such a way that they encapsulate functions of the Shortstack API or the Safe-sec Chip Orion Stack API. Since only Saf-sec Chip 1 is connected to the LON, the network access layer is not implemented on Saf-sec Chip 2. Another part of the first safety-security firmware layer is the saf-sec chip interface that handles data exchange between both saf-sec chips. It includes a hardware dependent driver and a software API that interfaces with the safety-security layer. It offers a function to send data to and receive data from the corresponding saf-sec chip.

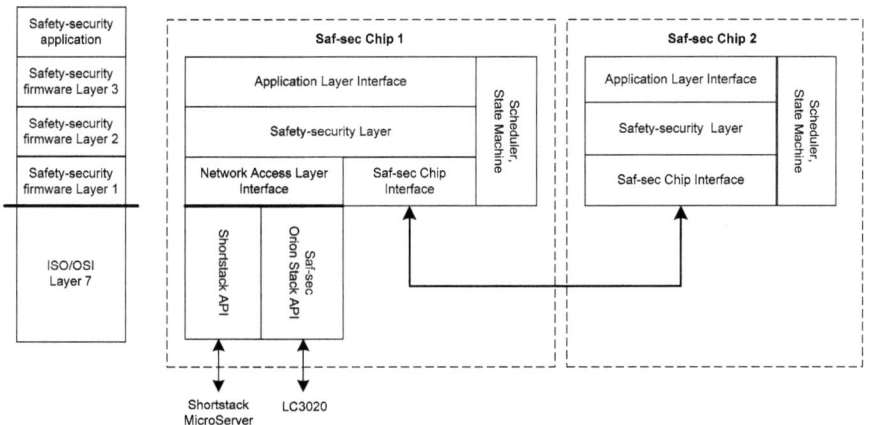

Fig. 9-2 Software design of safe-secure node

The *safety-security layer* is located in the middle of the software design and it comprises all software functionality directly referring to safety-security. It is interfacing with the application layer interface, and the network access layer interface and saf-sec chip interface. The safety-security layer is surrounded by two other layers, in other words, the safety-security firmware is separated into three layers, to make it absolutely independent from the third-party software. Second, the third layer is specified to hide safety-security functionality from the application programmer. Such a layer eases programming and avoids misuse of safety-security functions since it must be assumed that application programmers are not familiar with details of the firmware functionality.

The safety-security firmware layer 2 consists of multiple parts related to safety-security, i.e. primary functions: online self test module, safety related input/output module, software monitoring, or safe-secure protocol stack. Other parts are supporting the desired functionality called supporting functions like the smartcard interface. Albeit not part of layer 2, the scheduler and state machine, and the saf-sec chip interface are also supporting functions.

The *online self test* module includes online tests that are executed to guarantee a high integrity of the hardware by revealing faults in the different parts of the hardware. Tests are separated into volatile memory (RAM), non-volatile read only memory (FLASH), and CPU tests. In [TAM07] implementation examples are presented. In [WRA07, pp. 203] different test algorithms are outlined.

In general, volatile memory test algorithms differ in test effort and diagnostic coverage. A high test effort and a high diagnostic coverage is ensured when using the galloping pattern test, a low one when implementing the marching bit test [HOE86, pp. 7-50]. The level of the diagnostic coverage depends on the faults revealed by the test. Test with a high level detect faults according to the DC-fault model others only detect stuck-at faults (see subchapter 4.1).

Tests of the non-volatile read only memory rely on parity bits, checksums or CRCs [WRA07, pp. 213] whereas diagnostic coverage of the first is low and the last is high. To withstand intentional attacks also, the CRC is replaced by a MAC. The non-volatile memory is grouped in blocks of 256 byte. A 8 byte static MAC_{static} is calculated using the data of the block and stored for each block in a defined area in the EEPROM before installation. During operation the data is read from the memory periodically and a $MAC_{dynamic}$ is calculated on the smartcard and compared with MAC_{static} stored in the EEPROM. A matching of the MAC_{static} and $MAC_{dynamic}$ indicates that the integrity is granted. Storing the static MAC_{static} in the EEPROM of the smartcard is not required because it is a assumed that a MAC is calculated in a way so that it meets requirements mentioned in subchapter 1.3. Hence, it is not susceptible to brute-force attacks with reasonable computational effort.

Safety-related input/output module is responsible for testing the inputs and outputs, and to provide functionality to set/reset an input and to get the value of an output. Testing of the safe I/Os has to be synchronized between the saf-sec chips. In contrast to the aforementioned online self tests, safe I/O tests are performed in close cooperation between the saf-sec chips. Hardware schematics are designed in such a way that inputs signal is received and output signal set by both chips, and that test signals can be sent from one chip and received and evaluated by the other chip. As a consequence, a software function of the module triggers a test pulse on the first saf-sec chip and a software function on the other saf-sec chip checks if the test pulse has been received.

The objective of *software monitoring* is to ensure software integrity being part of the systematic integrity, in contrast to self tests that care for the hardware integrity. It is a means to detect if safety-security functions located in the volatile memory were executed according specification or have been altered due to unauthorized modification. Such misbehavior is possible because of software faults during the design or implementation, and exploitation of design and implementation vulnerabilities by attackers, respectively.

Software monitoring can be distinguished between time based and logic based monitoring [HOE86, pp. 7-86]. Both are integrated into the safe-secure firmware. The first type uses a timer with an independent time base. Typically, such a timer is called watchdog timer and realized in hardware. So software functions are monitored by measuring the execution time. After completion of a function the watchdog is reset by a software command. If the execution takes too long, the watchdog is triggered and predefined actions are taken. The type of monitoring is integrated to check if the system is blocked or modified in a way so that execution takes much longer than expected.

Logic based monitoring is used to check if functions have not been bypassed. Therefore, a counter is implemented that is increased every time the function was executed. Such a counter is available for every safety-security function. The counter values are exchanged within fixed periods of time between the saf-sec chips to detect a fault in the firmware. If the counter values are not equal on both saf-sec chips, predefined actions are taken.

Software Realization

The *safe-secure protocol stack* incorporates functionality to send and receive sensor/actuator data in a safe-secure way. Additionally, is supports network management activities such as configuring a node or exchanging security audit data, and handles the key update procedure of keys applied for security operations. The message structure used for the different tasks is shown in Fig. 9-3.

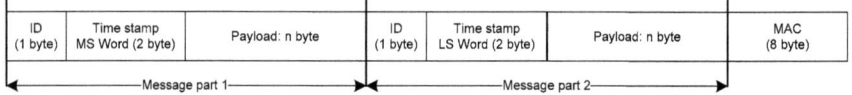

Fig. 9-3 Safe-secure message structure

A safe-secure message consists of two parts in order to detect multiple integrity faults. Moreover, a message authentication code (MAC) is added to the message to increase the level of data integrity and as a means to verify authenticity. Each message part starts with a one byte ID. The lower six bits give information on the length. The upper two bits are used to identify the message: sensor/actuator message without (00), network management message (01), key update message (10), network time synchronization message (11). Both message parts include a two byte timestamp: the first the upper two bytes, the second the lower two bytes of the four byte timestamp. Such a design allows message parts of equal length and hence a symmetric implementation of the stack. The size of the payload field can vary from one to sixty four (2^6) byte. Payload field itself is structured according to the message type.

In case of sending a sensor value each saf-sec chip build message part 1 and message part 2 and calculates the MAC. Saf-sec Chip 1 receives the complete message from the other chip and compares the whole message. If the MACs and the two message parts are identical, the message is sent otherwise discarded. Consequently, faulty messages due to a node internal failure are not sent. That avoids a waste of bandwidth and saves computational resources on receiver side since it need not to process the faulty message.

On receiver side the message is forwarded from Saf-sec Chip 1 to Saf-sec Chip 2 and processed by both (two channel structure): first the MAC is checked in order to verify integrity and authenticity, second the timestamp is used to check for insertion, repetition and wrong sequence of a message, third the payload field is compared bit by bit to detect other integrity failures not being revealed by the MAC. Results on the checks are exchanged between both saf-sec chips. Only if both agree on a positive result, the payload is released for further processing for example by the application software.

The *smartcard interface* handles data exchange between saf-sec chip and smartcard. As mentioned before, smartcards in general and the data transfer in particular are standardized in ISO 7816 [ISO78]. Consequently, the driver of the interface has to be realized in accordance with the standard specification. The API of the smartcard interface formats the massages. The structure of messages is also standardized in ISO 7816: so called application protocol data units (APDU) are specified to send a request and receive a response [NOV05, pp. 39].

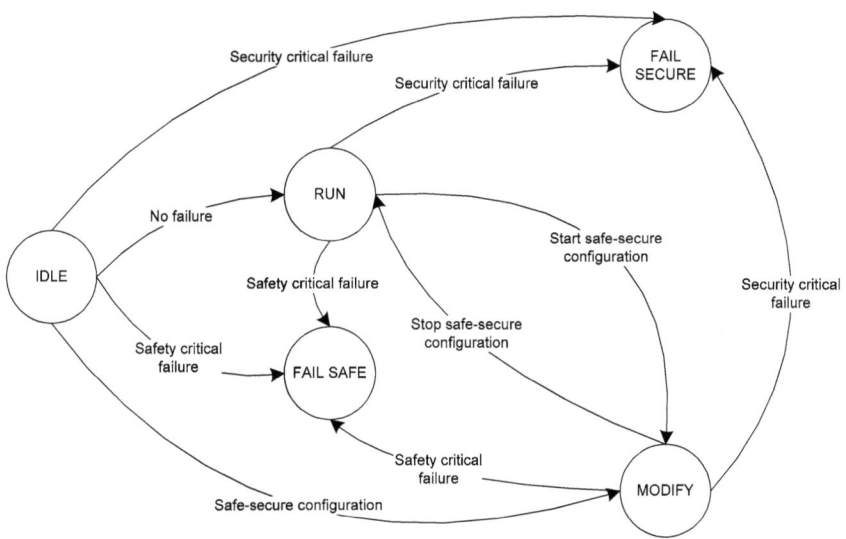

Fig. 9-4 Overview of safe-secure state machine

Safety-security functions must be called and executed on a regular base. For that reason a *scheduler* and a *state machine* are included in the firmware. To avoid computational overhead, to ease the integration of safety-security requirements and to reduce the likelihood of vulnerabilities, no commercial operating system is used. However, a static scheduling mechanism is realized with a fixed cycle time and a static sequence of functions, i.e. a single task scheduling. Such an approach first of all ensures a deterministic timing behavior. It guarantees that test pulses are sent or the RAM test is executed in fixed time intervals that cannot be ensured for example by the earliest-deadline-first scheduling mechanism [WOL01, pp. 377]. Second, static scheduling eases synchronization between saf-sec chips mandatory for the close cooperation between the saf-sec chips. Both chips start at the same time with the execution of function in the same order.

The state machine controls the behavior of the node. According to inputs received, it decides to which state to switch to. In a safe-secure node five states are specified as illustrated in Fig. 9-4. After a reset the node is in IDLE state and runs through the startup procedure. For example, the hardware is tested, the hardware interfaces are initialized and configuration parameters are copied from the smartcard to the RAM due to performance reasons. In case of no error the node enters to the RUN state where the node is operating. If security critical failures occur, the node enters FAIL SECURE state and if safety critical failures are detected, the node switches to FAIL SAFE state. In both states the functionality of the node is limited to a minimum that does not jeopardize security or safety. Both fail states are only left when the critical fault was eliminated by an operator. MODIFY state is used to configure the node, e.g. to make a safe-secure binding or to update keys. In the state the node provides only such functionality necessary to execute configuration requests and send the responses.

9.3 Development and Testing

Development of the firmware means implementation of the software design onto the target hardware by means of a programming language. That is, each primary and supporting safety-security function corresponds with a software module and is implemented by various software units or also called software functions. The result is source code for the saf-sec chips and the smartcard. During and after development firmware has to be tested in order to check that it complies with the software requirements. Additionally, tests are performed to validate that the behavior of the firmware accords with the intended use.

Safety-security related firmware is developed by using standard tools and standard programming languages. In addition, the firmware is uploaded to a commercial-off-the-shelf microcontroller. To ensure a level of safety-security, hardware is tested and guidelines for firmware development are specified. Such guidelines relate to organizational topics, the programming of code and test issues. They are a collection of 'best practices' and can be found in safety [HOE86, WRA07] as well as in the security domain [MCG06]. Examples of organizational guidelines are 'Use of only one version of a compiler and linker' or 'Use of a compiler that is proven in use' where list of possible bugs is available. Programming guidelines for example say 'Functions of a software module shall start with the same prefix'. Or, 'Choose meaningful and unambiguous names for functions and variables'. Other rules cover technical issues.

A rule concerning technical issues mentioned in [HOE86, pp. 4-7] says 'Consider carefully interrupts against polling'. With reference to the safety related inputs the rule means the following. As a matter of fact, sensor input signals will not be triggered synchronously, but asynchronously. In other words, in most cases it is not predicable when an input signal is available. Consequently, the inputs are supervised by an interrupt service routine (ISR). It is a software artifact that is called by the interrupt controller of the saf-sec chip every time a new input value is available. The new value is read from a hardware register and stored in a buffer as specified in the interrupt service routine. The ISR is called in parallel to the execution of the firmware. It requires computational power and slows down execution of software functions. If the input value changes permanently due to a maybe intentional disturbance on the input line, ISR is called constantly and the node cannot perform its functionality.

Another way of managing the problem is to poll the hardware register. Therefore an explicit software function is used that is called periodically by the scheduler. It reads the hardware register and for example stores the value in a software buffer. Such an approach is not susceptible to any disturbance of the input line. As a consequence, influence on the behavior of the node from the outside is reduced. The disadvantage of polling the safety related input register is that is time critical: the software function has to be called at least as often as a change of the input value is expected which is a strict timing constraint to be considered during implementation of the scheduler.

A further topic to be investigated is the use of dynamic memory allocation. The safe-secure protocol stack necessitates software buffers to store the message received for processing them and to store intermediate results while waiting for the result of message verification from the other saf-sec chip. The buffers can be declared as static arrays at startup or as dynamic arrays during operation and when needed. On the assumption that not all software buffers are needed at the same time, the use of dynamic memory allocation results in less memory consumption. In the light of limited resources on embedded devices the fact is welcomed. On the other hand, declaring static arrays at startup leads to a fixed code size already known before operation and delivered for example by the linker. Consequently, required memory resources can be estimated quite exactly – single variables in functions are not static. It is not possible that memory for a buffer cannot be allocated or memory cells are overwritten and protected resources are modified. Moreover, static buffers need not be released after use in contrast to dynamic buffers. In case of a frequent use of dynamic buffers it is likely that the resource is not freed, freed and used again afterwards or freed twice which leads to a failure.

What also has to be considered during implementation is to check the return value of functions. In general, it is absolutely recommended to declare all functions in such a way that they return a value. Unchecked return values can cause to overlook unexpected states or conditions. An obvious example is the RAM test. In case of a revealed fault leading to a safety critical failure, an error code is returned. Not checking the value results in not switching to FAIL SAFE state and therefore safety of the node is endangered. Another example is the access control. It is verified if a message of a producer is accepted or not. A return value gives information whether the producer is authorized.

Finally, the most security critical topic is a buffer overflow. In the case it is written outside the bounds of allocated memory regardless if static or dynamic. Thus, data is corrupted, the node firmware crashes or malicious payload is executed. Such a problem might occur in a application layer interface function. A function to write sensor data into a 16 byte buffer is offered to the application programmer. Parameter of the function is a pointer to the data and the length of data. The pointer, however, points to a 20 byte data field and length of data is set to 20 byte. Inside the application layer interface function the data bytes are copied into the 16 byte buffer. To avoid a buffer overflow, length of data received must always be verified if it is less than or equal 16 byte. An error code is returned if data length is greater than 16 byte and data is not processed. In case of an attack data length maybe set deliberately to 16 byte or less. Again, buffer overflow is avoided, but data is processed.

Beside organizational and programming guidelines also guidelines for testing are available. The firmware is tested first to verify and second to validate the software artifact. Testing the firmware means uncovering bugs for removal, but not to prove that firmware is error free. It is absolutely a necessity to test the firmware because complete avoidance of human mistakes during coding is not realistic. According to [WAN05] the probability of a fault for a well-trained and experienced programmer in software code is about 1%. Put another way, there is an error in every 100 statements coded. Additionally, it must be mentioned that testing is a very good means to *detect* errors. On the other hand, a defined level of safety and security also requires further means such as well documented source code or well structured software specifications. In other words, supporting lifecycle activities help to *avoid* faults during programming of source code.

Testing is an important part of software development and an area under investigation for many years in the software engineering discipline, for example in [ZUS01, pp. 191]. A lot of terms are in use in the area of testing that are mixed up or classified differently. Fig. 9-5 provides a way of classifying terms related to testing.

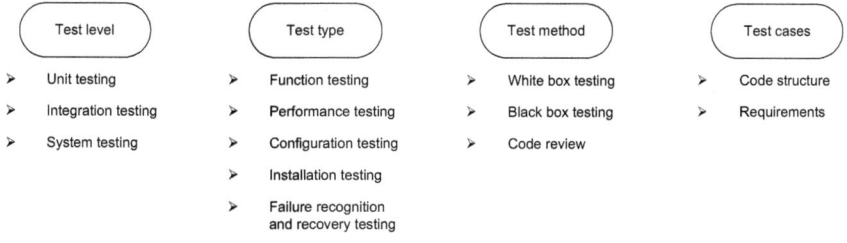

Fig. 9-5 Classification of terms related to testing

First, tests are carried out to check small pieces of the software artifact like units or modules. For example, testing the RAM test implemented as a software module as mentioned in [AMA07] is a module test. Or, testing the software unit used to process a message received, is also a unit test. Second, integration of software modules or units and testing them is called integration testing. E.g., integration of units of the safe-secure protocol stack in order to trigger a request and receive a response. Integration testing also means migrating the software to the target hardware and performing tests. Finally, system testing stands for testing the complete software running on the target hardware of the node. That is, software modules like RAM test, safe-secure protocol, or safety related inputs and outputs are integrated onto each saf-sec chip and are tested for different criteria such as performance or functionality.

Test types differ in the test objective, i.e. what is the focus of testing. They can be carried out at the different test levels. Fig. 9-5 lists some examples of function testing. The intention of the test type function testing is to verify if the requirements are met by the developed software. For example, the safe-secure protocol stack receives a message from an invalid producer. If the message is discarded and an appropriate error code is returned, the test was performed successfully. Or, a fault was introduced into the RAM. If the RAM test does not reveal the stuck-at fault, the test failed.

Another test is the performance test in which response times, transaction rates, and other time sensitive requirements are measured and evaluated. The goal of the performance test is to check that performance requirements have been achieved under different workloads. E.g., a change of a safety related input is recognized within 3 ms. Or, the node receives valid messages permanently and it is verified if all messages have still been processed according to expectation. Such tests are called stress tests or load tests.

Penetration testing is a security related test technique. The test objective is to determine how the node behaves under attack. As written in [MCG06, p. 172], penetration testing is 'testing for negatives'. Derived from identified security risks during specification, tests are performed to reveal vulnerabilities. E.g., a message with invalid length is sent to the node and is check if a buffer overflow in the network access layer interface is handled properly. Penetration testing is about testing the firmware on the node hardware, i.e. it is carried out at the end of software development.

Installation testing has two purposes. The first is to ensure that the software can be installed under different conditions – such as installations where just a small/large number of producers and consumers is specified – under normal and abnormal conditions. Abnormal conditions include insufficient memory, data transmission errors, and wrong parameter settings. The second purpose is to verify that, once installed, the software operates correctly. This usually means running a number of the tests that were developed for function testing.

Failure recognition and recovery testing ensures that the firmware can successfully identify failures, react properly and recover from a variety of hardware, software or network malfunctions with undue loss of data or data integrity. Recovery testing is an antagonistic test process in which the application or system is exposed to extreme conditions, or simulated conditions, to cause a failure. Automatically and manually triggered recovery processes are invoked, and the application or system is monitored and inspected to verify proper application, or system, and data recovery has been achieved. It is similar to penetration testing, but the focus is not only on malicious attacks. For example, it is tested if the missing of heartbeats from a defined producer is recognized and if the consumer enters fail safe state; moreover, if the consumer leaves fail safe state after heartbeats have been received again.

The various test types can be executed by means of different test methods. The white box testing considers the software as a transparent box [WAN05]. The test type focuses on the inner structure of the firmware. Tests are designed in such a way that all statements in a unit are executed once (C_0), or every branch (C_1) or each logical path (C_2) is run through. Put another way, white box tests differ in the test coverage (C) [HOW87].

Black box testing treats the firmware like a black box. According to the requirements specification it is verified if correct corresponding output values to input values are created. Whereas white box tests are applied for small software artifacts like parts of the RAM test or the receiving function of the safe-secure protocol stack, black box tests are performed in case of integration and systems tests.

Code review is a static test approach that can be carried out either manually or automatically. Manual code review is executed by experts together with the development team. Automatic code review is supported by tools that analyze the code. Both ways are concentrating on topics like: Is the code programmed according to the coding guidelines? Are the functions well documented? Does every if-command also have a else-command? Is the interface between the layers clearly specified and implemented accordingly? In [MCG06, pp. 123] code review tools are mentioned and presented.

Every test type is based on test cases. Such test cases specify the target test item (safety related input/output module or state machine), give a description of the test case, specify the expected result and the test data to be used. There are two possible ways to specify a test case: based on the requirements or derived from the code structure. The first one is applied in case of black box, the other in case of white box testing.

On developing safety-security related software all three test types mentioned in Fig. 9-5 should be applied to verify and validate the system. White box test require more effort compared to black box tests. Each unit might be tested with various test cases depending on the test coverage and the complexity. Faults can be located easier though because inner structure of the code is examined. In addition, white box tests are carried out by the programmers themselves since they are familiar with the structure of the source code. Black box tests, however, are performed by external testers to avoid that a wrong implementation and incorrect test cause a supposedly successful test result.

9.4 Installation and Operation

After validation and verification by means of test procedures the firmware is installed. In addition, an application software using functionality of the application layer interface has to be integrated. Some of the network configuration dependent parameter are specified and uploaded to the node. Next, the node is set into operation: hardware and software is initialized, and in the end the node is ready for providing its intended functionality. The following paragraphs concentrate on the installation and operation of *node* software whereas chapter 10 outlines such issues from a *system* point of view.

Table 9-1 Node software

Firmware	Application software (examples)	Configuration parameter	Cryptographic keys
Saf-sec Chip 1	Smoke detector	Producer related	Producer-consumer
Saf-sec Chip 2	Fire damper	Consumer related	Node-management device
	Emergency lighting	Application related	Node software integrity

In essence, node software consists of four parts as mentioned in Table 9-1. First of all, the firmware different for Saf-sec Chip 1 and Saf-sec Chip 2 due to the asymmetric hardware architecture is part of the node software. It provides the required safety-security functionality and consists of three layers as illustrated in Fig. 9-2.

On top of the firmware layers resides the application software. The piece of software specifies what the node is used for. In case of a fire alarm system application there are nodes with a smoke detector (sensor) application, others with a fire damper (actuator) application, or nodes having an emergency lighting (actuator) application installed. Some applications might be configurable by parameters. In the majority of the cases the application software is not realized by the same group being responsible for the development of the firmware. Nevertheless, the application software has also to be developed according to the requirements of the software safety-security lifecycle model.

Application software of a node necessitates ways to send its data and receive data from other nodes. Consequently, a number of producers to send and consumers to receive data in a safe-secure way is going to be specified. For example, the smoke detector application on a Node A uses two producers OUT_sd1 and OUT_sd2 (Fig. 9-6) to send sensor values received from two smoke detectors connected to the node. By contrast, the fire damper application on a Node C specifies four consumers IN_fd1 to IN_fd4 (Fig. 9-6) in order to receive messages from other nodes. According to the information in the messages the fire damper is closed or opened. The emergency lighting application on a Node B includes two consumers IN_el1 and IN_el2 (Fig. 9-6) since it is assumed that two emergency lights are connected to a node. Again, depending on the data received the light is turned on or switched off.

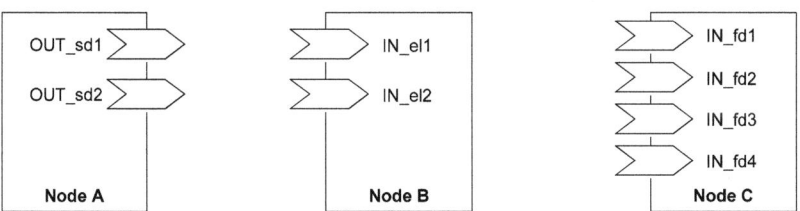

Fig. 9-6 Producer and consumer configuration

To ensure dedicated security objectives, cryptographic keys are used. Software mentioned before is located in the FLASH of the saf-sec chips. However, the firmware part referring to operations with cryptographic keys (e.g. MAC generation or verification) is stored on the smartcard. In addition, keys are stored on the smartcard to prevent them from disclosure. At least there are three types of keys: the ones used to secure communication between producer and consumer (each producer has its unique key), others to exchange messages between node and the management device, and keys to ensure integrity of node software stored in the FLASH of the saf-sec chips. Differentiating between different types of keys is necessary, otherwise revealing a key results in breaching security of the whole system. E.g., message from producer A to consumer B was analyzed and the key could be received from the analysis. As a consequence, all other producer-consumer messages are not secure anymore. And messages between network management device and nodes as well as node software integrity are not protected any longer.

Software being stored in the FLASH of the saf-sec chips is comprised in a single software image. As already outlined before, integrity of the software image has to be ensured during operation. Consequently, the image is separated into blocks of 256 byte. Each block is secured by a MAC by applying a dedicated key. The MAC generation is performed before installation and then MACs are stored at the end of the software image in the FLASH too. Assuming an image of about 60 Kbyte and a MAC of 8 byte, additional FLASH memory of 1920 byte is necessary.

The key to verify the MAC and check integrity of the software image is stored on the smartcard also before installation. Therefore, it need not be distributed over the network, yet security operation can be executed from the beginning of operation. Such an approach is called out-of-band initialization. The approach is also used to store keys to guarantee a secure communication between network management device and every node at initialization.

After every node was equipped with the proper software, it is installed and ready for operation. Every node runs through a startup procedure as shown in Fig. 9-7. Note, that during startup of the node safety-security must always be ensured. The startup procedure is started after pressing the reset button on the node. Next, the hardware is initialized, i.e. the interrupt and exception vectors are configured, the watchdog timer is set up and the like. Then the complete RAM is tested, the CPU checked and the MACs in the FLASH are compared with the ones calculated online on the smartcard. If the tests are passed successfully, the safety related inputs and outputs are configured, and initialized with the predefined safe state value. As a further step the hardware interfaces are set up, i.e. the smartcard and saf-sec chip interface, and the interface to the EN 14908 chip are set into operation. In case of succeeding in initializing the hardware interfaces, network configuration data is read from the smartcard and copied into volatile buffers in the RAM due to performance reasons. Finally, diagnostic information including security audit data stored on the smartcard is analyzed. The information also includes the last state of the node before reset. According to the information the node is set to RUN, MODIFY, FAIL SAFE or FAIL SECURE state.

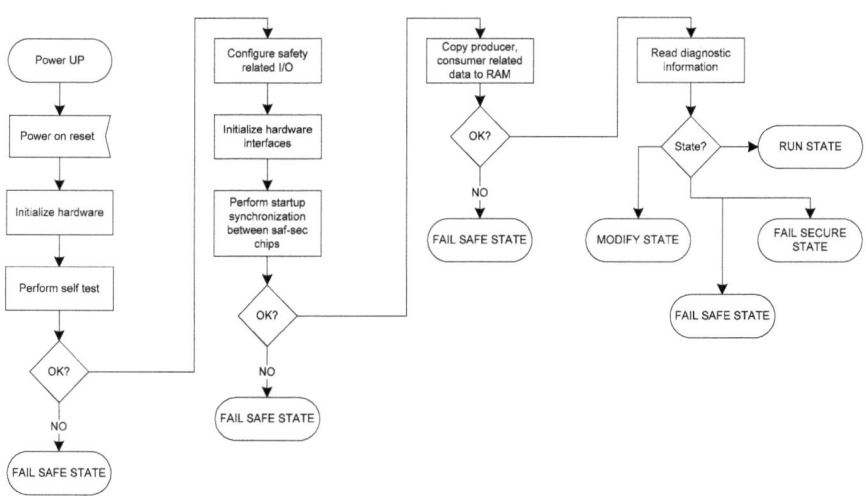

Fig. 9-7 Safe-secure startup procedure

During the whole startup procedure no messages are processed and input values coming from the safety related inputs are ignored. And the safety-security application software is not executed. Put another way, the node does not react to any external input nor does it produce any output. In addition, the safety-security firmware does not react to inputs from the application. Thus, the node cannot be influenced by malicious attacks from the outside. Second, the complete hardware is tested as well as the software stored in the FLASH. Consequently, integrity of the node is guaranteed. Finally, the node returns to the same state before reset. By doing so, it is impossible to change for example from a FAIL SECURE state entered after a deliberate modification of the software to RUN state and full operation by just resetting the node.

10. System Integration

The intention of the chapter is to present a way of integrating a *node* into a building automation and control system (BACS) in a safe-secure way. Integration in the context means discussing the procedure of configuring and maintaining a safe-secure node in a BACS. Related topics are establishing communication paths between producer and consumers, or key distribution and key updates. It is not meant to examine the topic integration in a broader context as mentioned for example in [SAU05] where the three major aspects of integration are presented and discussed: horizontal, vertical and temporal integration.

As shown in Fig. 2-1, a typical architecture of a BACS consists of three levels: the public network at the top, the private in the middle and the field level network at the bottom. The characteristic of every level is mentioned in subchapter 2.1. Different entities are located in the networks. Beside the nodes there a two other entities relevant for safety-security considerations: the gateway and the network management device.

10.1 Gateway and Network Management Device

The field level network, and private and public network are separated by dedicated entities, referred to as *gateways* in the thesis. Gateways provide a suitable protocol conversion between an IP-based private or public network, and a specific fieldbus protocol [LOB05, p. 11]. Often the gateway is going to have caching mechanism for a set of data objects to ease data exchange with clients in the outside world [PAL00]. The gateway is the entrance point to the field level. It makes remote access to the field level network possible. Hence, it is also called *access point* [REY05].

The gateway is not safety relevant and it is absolute transparent from a safety point of view when it does not interpret the payload of messages, but can contribute a lot to the security of the field level network. It is part of the 'black channel' assuming that it does not process safety related data. It receives a message, stores it temporarily, converts the received message into the other protocol and forwards it. That is, the gateway increases the transmission delay. Therefore measures are applied such as a timestamp and watchdog to detect too long delays [WRA05]. However, the gateway does not intentionally change or process the data, or acts according to specific data value.

Situation is different in case of security. Attaching field level networks to IP-based networks exposes the field level network to all kind of attacks that are common on the Internet nowadays. However, as outlined in chapter 3 when examining standard BACS, very little security functionality except BACnet is integrated. Therefore a lot of research has been made so far to increase security of field level networks. In general, there are two approaches: the integration of standard Internet security measures into the field level network as presented in [TRE04]. The various network levels are considered to be a single security zone.

Second, it is possible to divide the BACS into two security zones: the field level, and the IP-based private and public zone. In the IP-based zone standard Internet security measures are used whilst other measures are applied in the field level, referred to as smartcard approach in [PAL00]. In that case, the gateway not only converts the protocol, but also converts the security measures and must be considered to be security critical. In addition, the gateway can also check during security measure conversion if a message is allowed to access the field level network by means of an access control. In general, the gateway can be enhanced with security features such as a firewall [PAL00] to be a security related gateway so that is defeats attacks from the outside. It is important to mention that a security related gateway does not prevent from attacks coming from the inside. Hence, it supports security, but does not alone guarantee the security of the BACS.

The two security zone is assumed in the following example: standard Internet security measures to secure the safe-secure message in the IP-based networks and the use of symmetric ciphers with private keys stored on smartcards in the field level network. On the other hand, Internet security measures would have to be implemented on the nodes, but they are rather resource consuming [PAL00]. They often use asymmetric ciphers that add more overhead to a message and require more computational power compared to symmetric ciphers. Implementation of Internet security measures reduces the field of application of a safe-secure BACS because transmission time and processing time of messages on the node is increased. Consequently, the reaction time is lowered.

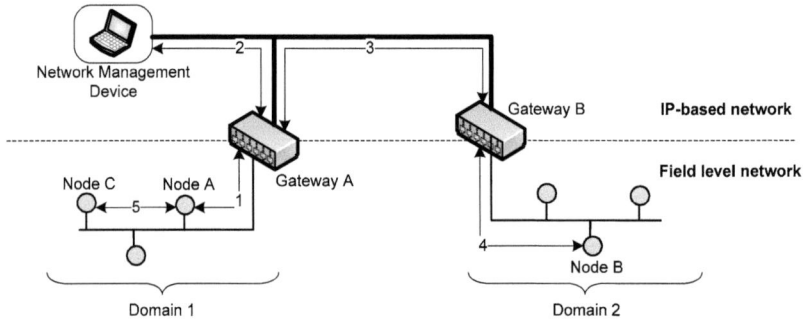

Fig. 10-1 Communication in a safe-secure BACS

The consequences of the two security zone approach are illustrated in Fig. 10-1: The key used to secure messages between network management device and node (path 1 and 2) must also be stored securely on the gateway. The reason is the following. The network management device and the gateway share a secure communication path 2 granted by Internet security measures. The network management device wants to send an authenticated request to Node A using the key $K_{MD,A}$. It uses the secure path 2 to the gateway. The gateway, however, must verify whether the message is allowed to access the field level network. Therefore, it takes the private key of Node A $K_{MD,A}$ and checks the MAC. In case of a successful check the message is forwarded to Node A (path 1). The node also must verify the authenticity of the message with its private key $K_{MD,A}$. Node A sends a response by using the private key $K_{MD,A}$. The gateway receives the message and checks the MAC and only forwards it if the check was successful. Finally, the network management device receives the message and can verify if the message is coming from Node A.

Moreover, the keys of producers and consumers on various nodes that are exchanging messages from Domain 1 to Domain 2 and vice versa (path 1, 3, 4) have to be available on the Gateway A and Gateway B for the same reason mentioned above. Keys used for message exchange between producer of Node A and consumer of Node C (path 5) being part of the same domain need not be stored on the gateway, though.

To sum up, the gateway is transparent from the safety point of view (assuming safety related data is not processed), but not from the security point of view. So safe-secure message exchange is between node and gateway (path 1), gateway and network management device (path 2). Or between producer and consumer residing in different domains: Node A to Gateway A (path 1), Gateway A to Gateway B (path 3), and Gateway B to Node B (path 4).

The network management device is connected to the private, but is accessible from the public network and exchanges messages via gateways (Fig. 2-1). Such devices as the name suggests are used to manage the network by applying standard management tools. For management and maintenance it is advantageous to have unlimited access to resources, but it is a big security risk, especially when having free access to application and configuration data [SCH02, REY05]. A possible solution to the problem is to use tools limiting the access to the nodes according to rights of the operator by means of access control mechanism [SCH02].

In a safe-secure BACS the problem is solved differently. Safe-secure messages received via the network access unit (EN 14908 chip) are stored in a table in the ISO/OSI Layer 7 (Fig. 9-2), called the layer-7-table. Standard network management tools can read and write application data in the layer-7-table. Data in the table, however, has not been processed by safety-security firmware yet. The data is equal to the one sent over the network. Only if integrity and authenticity is granted, the data is copied to a table of the safe-secure software, called the ALI-table. Theses values are used by the application. If application triggers a sending process, it writes into the ALI-table and that data is used in the message to be sent. The complete safe-secure message is finally copied into the layer-7-table to forward it unchanged to the network access unit. In other words, the standard network management tools do not have direct access to the ALI-table and therefore cannot write or read safety-security related data without being recognized.

To ensure a safe-secure access to safety-security related data, standard network management tools are enhanced with additional libraries or plug-ins as presented in

[FIS07] for SafetyLon. The enhanced software manages the producer and consumer related parameters, application parameters, and cares for a secure storing of the cryptographic keys. The design of such a tool is beyond the scope of the thesis. However, as much information is conveyed to understand the configuration, commissioning and maintenance of a node.

10.2 Node Configuration and Commissioning

Each node in the field level network must be configured so that it is able send message to other nodes and receive messages from nodes in a safe-secure way. As a result, producer and consumer related configuration parameter must be sent to the different nodes by the network management device. And cryptographic keys are distributed to the nodes. If required, also application related parameters are transferred to the node. In the following, it is assumed that the node is ready for operation as mentioned in subchapter 9.4; additionally, the producer consumer communication relies on network variable service (NV), and network management device to node communication is based on explicit message service.

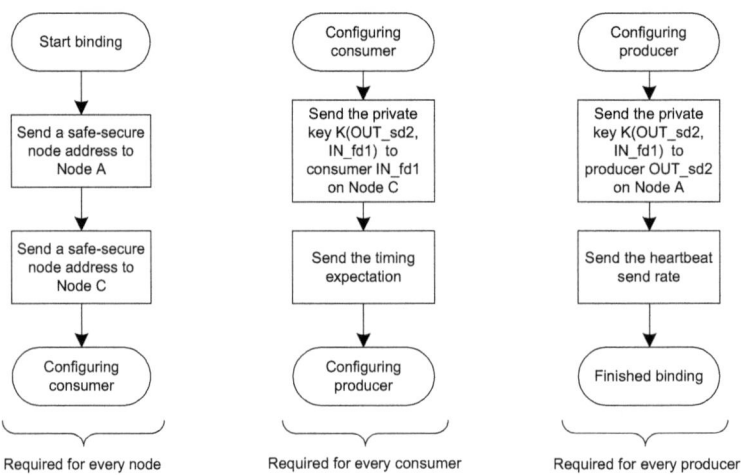

Fig. 10-2 Safe-secure binding example

Node configuration consists of two major steps: first the standard afterwards the safety-security related configuration. And it is executed by sending requests from the network management device to the corresponding nodes. Standard network configuration with NVs is called binding. Each NV on a node has a unique index, already defined before installation of the node software. Theses indices are used to establish logic communication paths among nodes. Applying the names mentioned in Fig. 9-6, the NV OUT_sd2 with index 2 of type output is bound to the NV IN_fd1 with index 4 of type input.

Next the safe-secure binding is executed. In the process output NVs are referred to as producers and input NVs as consumers. In the following the safe-secure binding is explained on the basis of an example: Node A includes the producer OUT_sd2, and Node C the consumer IN_fd1 (Fig. 9-6). First, every node is assigned a safe-secure address in order to identify the node clearly as shown in Fig. 10-2. The address is different from the standard network identifier (NID) and used within every safe-secure network management message. Without a safe-secure address the node does not respond to any message except the one that includes the safe-secure address.

Second, the consumer receives the private key $K_{OUT\_sd2,\ IN\_fd1}$, which it always uses to check security of messages received from the corresponding producer. Besides, the value of the timing expectation is set by the user. The value specifies the maximum time that can go by before the watchdog timer is triggered. Put another way, it is the maximum allowed time interval between two valid messages from the corresponding producer. If the watchdog was triggered, the consumer switches to a predefined fail safe state. As outlined in Table 8-2, the watchdog is utilized to detect malfunctions on producer side or of the network access unit, or to detect the loss of messages. The lower the value, the faster malfunctions and loss of message are detected. That is, the value specifies the maximum fault detection time. Though, the size of the value must be specified in correspondence with the delays on the nodes and the network. A too low value may decrease availability of the consumer. E.g., each nodes requires 300 ms to process a message, delay on the network is about 300 μs and negligible. Total delay is 600 ms. A timing expectation value of 700 ms would results in the fact that if just a single message was lost, the consumer enters fail safe state.

Third, the producer is configured on Node A. It also receives the private key $K_{OUT\_sd2,\ IN\_fd1}$ which is exercised to protect data sent to the consumer. Additionally, the value of the heartbeat send rate is transferred to the producer. The value is a multiple of the timing expectation. The factor used is equal to the number of messages that can be lost before the consumer enters fail safe state. I.e., a timing expectation on consumer side of 3 s would cause a heartbeat send rate of 1 s on the assumption that 2 messages can get lost.

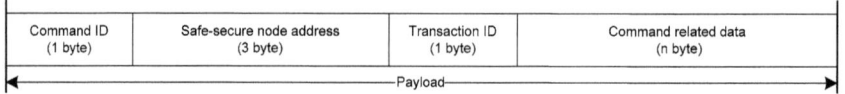

Fig. 10-3 Payload field of a safe-secure network management message

The safe-secure binding in particular and network management activities in general like sending application related parameters rely on a three step request/response mechanism, called a transaction. Request and response messages are formatted as shown in Fig. 9-3 and secured by a private key unique for each node and network management connection. That is, every node in the field level network shares a key with the network management device. To guarantee secure communication from initialization phase on, the keys are distributed out-of-band before installation and are stored on a smartcard as outlined in subchapter 9.4. In accordance with [FIS07] the payload field in the safe-secure message is structured as illustrated in Fig. 10-3.

To give details on the transaction mechanism the command 'Configuring of a producer – Send the heartbeat send rate' from Fig. 10-2 is taken as an example.

1. Verify that the right node is addressed. The management device sends a request to the node with the safe-secure address of the node, authenticated with the appropriate key and asking the node for a 'Start transaction'.
The node checks authenticity and the node address. Moreover, it checks whether a transaction is open or not. Only a single transaction can be opened since just one network management device is allowed to configure the node. If all checks were passed successfully, the node returns a response including a transaction ID – a counter value increased every time a new transaction is opened. Consequently, each transaction can be distinguished.

2. Perform the network management command. In case of a successful response, the device is ensured that it is the right node to be configured. The device sends a request with the command ID 'Set heartbeat send rate' and the transaction ID received to the node. Furthermore, the heartbeat send rate

and the NV index of the producer and a $MAC_{heartbeat}$ calculated with the key of the producer $K_{OUT\_sd2,\ IN\_fd1}$ over the heartbeat send rate value is included in the command related data.

The node receives the message and first checks authenticity of the message. On success, it verifies the $MAC_{heartbeat}$ of the corresponding producer. If authenticity is granted, the heartbeat send value is stored in a buffer, and not yet written into the corresponding table for producer and consumer related data. Received data that was copied into the buffer is returned to the device in the response message. If sent and received command related data is equal the device is sure that the right data is on the node.

3. Test in case of a write command that network management data was written successfully on the node. The device sends a request with the 'Commit transaction' so that the network management command takes effect.

On receiving the request the node writes the heartbeat send rate value to the table for producer and consumer related data located in the RAM. As mentioned in subchapter 9.4, the data is copied from the smartcard to the RAM due to performance reasons. Additionally, the heartbeat send rate value is written into the smartcard and read back afterwards. The data is placed into the response message to the device. If command related data in the response message is also equal to the one included in the command request, it is guaranteed that heartbeat send rate value has been written and the command was executed successfully. With the 'Commit transaction' response the transaction is closed automatically.

After configuration of the nodes, they are set into RUN state by the network management device. At this point of the time, the node still does not react to any incoming message or sensor input. It only tries to synchronize its time based on a centralized or decentralized approach [SEV07, pp. 24]. Finally, the node is time synchronized and configured, and start to process messages.

10.3 Node Operation and Maintenance

A lot of topics relating to operation and maintenance of the system in general were presented in subchapter 9.4. Maintenance is concerned with activities like reconfiguration of the network, replacement and installation of additional nodes. All the activities rely on the same mechanism as presented before in subchapter 10.2. Hence, they are not outlined again.

Key update mechanism, however, is different from the initial key distribution. The basics were discussed in subchapter 6.3. There are multiple approaches like the one presented in [NOV05, pp. 49] or [GRA05, pp. 132]. In [SCH01] a security architecture including key update mechanism is presented for an BACS connected to the Internet. Generally, key updating is a sophisticated task and detailed discussion is out of the scope of the thesis.

In the following, operation of the system is highlighted. In particular, safe-secure communication between two nodes is outlined as shown in Fig. 10-4 is taken as an example. Node A runs the smoke detector application and includes the producer OUT_sd2. Sensor 2 is connected to the safety related input. Node C is equipped with the fire damper application and the consumer IN_fd1. A fire damper 1 is plugged to the safety related output. Both nodes were configured properly (safe-secure binding) as described in subchapter 10.2, network time synchronization was successful, and all saf-sec chips are in RUN state.

In case of smoke detected, the smoke detector sensor sends a signal to Node A. The signal is received by both saf-sec chips (S1,1 and S2,1) as illustrated in Fig. 10-4. On the assumption that the smoke detector application triggers a message sending process when a signal has been received, the sensor value is embedded into a safe-secure message on both saf-sec chips. Next, they send the message to the smartcards (S1,2 and S2,2) where the MAC with the appropriate key is calculated. In general, all operations that require cryptographic keys are performed on the smartcard to avert a disclosure of the keys. The smartcards return the complete safe-secure message structured as shown in Fig. 9-3 to the corresponding chip (S1,3 and S2,3). Since only Saf-sec Chip 1 is connected to the EN 14908 chip, Saf-sec Chip 2 sends its complete message to his neighboring chip (4). The result of the sending process is two safe-secure messages built in parallel on two chips being independent from each other. If the two messages are not identical, a failure in one of the chips must be assumed and the message is discarded. Hence, e.g. deliberate modification of the software on a chip can be detected. Finally, the message is sent to the EN 14908 chip (5) and transferred over the network.

The safe-secure message from Node A is received by Node C via the EN 14908 chip and sent to Saf-sec Chip 1 (1). It, in turn, forwards the complete message to Saf-sec Chip 2 (2). Next both chip perform the following task in parallel: the message is sent to the smartcards to verify authenticity and integrity (S1,3 and S2,3). The result is returned to the chips (S1,4 and S2,4). Furthermore, other checks are performed such as verification of timestamps. The final result of the various checks is exchanged between the saf-sec chips (5,6). If both agree on a positive end result, the fire damper application on each chip sets the safety related output (S1,7 and S2,7). Otherwise, the safe-secure message is discarded.

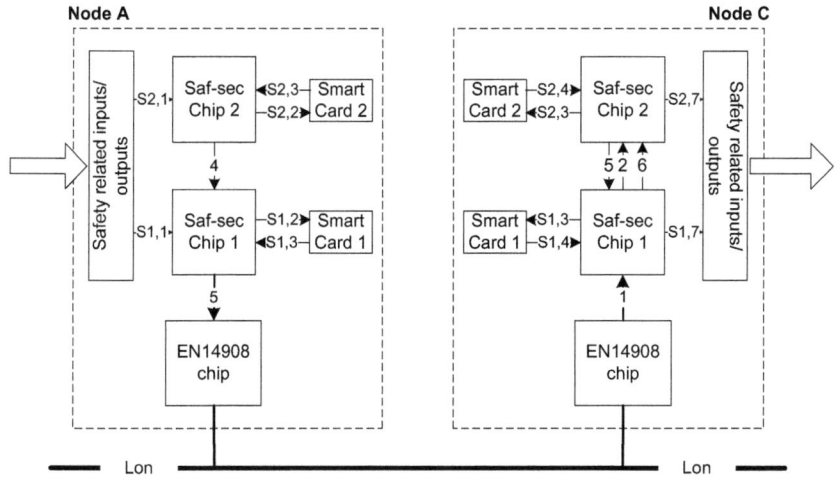

Fig. 10-4 Safe-secure communication between two nodes

Heartbeats, i.e. messages sent periodically to detect failures on the producer side or the network, are based on the same procedure. However, they are sent by Node A in defined time intervals and the application is not involved. The payload sent is the last valid one received from the sensor. By contrast, Node C processes the heartbeat the same way as mentioned before.

In conclusion, any input to a node either from a sensor or the network is processed on both saf-sec chips independently and results are crosschecked. The same is valid for every output generated (output to an actuator or network output). That is due to the required two channel architecture. All operations that necessitate cryptographic keys are executed on the smartcards to ensure a high level of security.

11. Conclusion and Outlook

The possibilities to gain synergies by taking an harmonized approach towards safety and security in BACS is given in many areas. This fact is honored often, e.g., "Safety and security [...] are closely related, and their similarities can be used to the advantage of both in terms of borrowing effective techniques from each to deal with the other." [LEV95]. Yet little effort to combine the fields is given because applications are thought to be either safety or security critical.

In [BUR92] it is stated that a system can be viewed as safety and security critical since systems can be seen from different points of view of course. That is especially true for the near future because IT-systems and also BAC systems are embedded in more and more influential parts of our living and working environment. And they are networked [PFI04]. For example, in building automation mainly for cost reasons a combination of formerly separated networks for safety, e.g., fire alarm system, security, e.g., access control, and operation, e.g. heating, ventilation and air conditioning, is desired.

As a consequence, the thesis presents a common approach of a harmonized safety *and* security BACS. Techniques such as the risk analysis common in both areas are synchronized to figure out hazards that endanger safety or security of a BACS. Since various hazards even jeopardize both safety and security of the system, a dual usage of countermeasures is feasible. The safety-security lifecycle model presented specifies requirements for the different stages in development and use of a BACS.

11.1 Results and Benefits

The thesis introduces a common approach to functional safety and system security in building automation and control systems (BACS). The approach has two objectives, namely to specify a way

1. how to integrate safety and security, and
2. how to develop and use a safe-secure BACS.

First, safety and security are harmonized, i.e. standard concepts and methodologies from both disciplines are applied and the focus is on the interaction between safety and security. Interaction in the context means areas are investigated where safety and security have identical or contradicting goals or requirements, or use identical or conflicting measures.

As a result, a *conflict resolution* approach and a *measure assessment* is introduced by the author. Such methods are necessary because not in every case safety will prevail over security. That may not be true seen from a system point of view – the complete system must always react so that life of people, and not protection of assets is ensured. However, on entity, hardware or software level the situation is different. Why should not a security requirement or measure instead of a safety one be used, e.g. a message authentication code (MAC) in lieu of a CRC and therefore also grant authenticity? There is no negative impact on safety itself, but on the reaction time since calculation of a CRC needs much less time than calculation of a MAC.

Conflict resolution is a means to handle conflicts on requirement level (Fig. 7-4). It specifies a rule based approach and a framework for conflict resolution. At the beginning a conflict resolution policy consisting of one to many rules is set up. Next, safety and security requirements are categorized in detective, corrective and preventive. Finally, the conflict resolution policy is applied to every corrective and preventive requirement. The outcome is a set of conflict free requirements that is verified by threat-hazard and risk analysis afterwards.

Measure assessment specifies a procedure of managing conflicts on function level. For that reason, measures are grouped into three classes: directly matching, unique and different effort. Whereas the first two do not show any interaction between safety and security, the third class does. Safety and security functional measures that require different effort, but are derived from the same requirement are assessed by using six factors, shown in Fig. 7-7. The result is that either the safety or the security measure is being implemented.

Second, a *safety-security lifecycle model* is developed (Fig. 6-1) that specifies a way of developing and using a safety-security related BACS. It gives requirements for the different activities in the system life, starting with the concept and ending with the decommissioning of the system. It is based on the safety lifecycle model included in the international standard IEC 61508. Moreover, the way of deriving security requirements and functions presented in Common Criteria (IEC 15408) is integrated into the lifecycle model. The result is the safety-security harmonized lifecycle model enhanced with activities like conflict resolution and measure assessment to cover the interaction between both areas.

The safety-security lifecycle model includes activities relating to the entities of the system, others corresponding to the system (Fig. 8-1). There are multiple entity lifecycles, one for a node, and another for a gateway, but just a single system lifecycle. Activities with the word 'overall' in the name are valid for the system, others for each entity.

The lifecycle model defines four primary processes, each one including activities that determine requirements *how* to develop and use the BACS. Additionally, it incorporates supporting processes (Table 5-1). As the name implies activities of the processes support the primary and organizational processes (management, infrastructure, improvement, and training). Activities of the supporting processes are invoked by the different activities of the primary processes multiple times. Organizational processes are the basis of the primary and supporting processes.

Both objectives are realized in such a way so that the common approach is accepted by safety experts, security practitioners, and BACS developers and operators. Consequently, the common approach is based on three international standards (Fig. 11-1), IEC 61508 covers safety related issues, Common Criteria (IEC 15408) security related issues, and IEC 12207 is the source of lifecycle related topics. In addition, it harmonizes safety and security in order not to specify new terminology and methodology, but add further activities to handle the interaction. Such activities are specified in a general manner, and intentionally avoid a very formal realization.

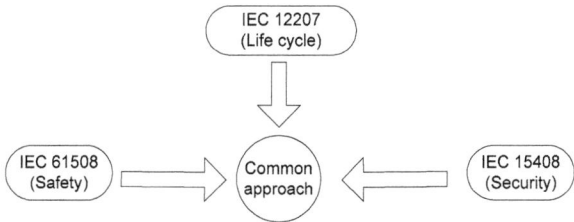

Fig. 11-1 Basis of common approach

The benefit of the common approach is different depending on the target audience. Developer and operator can apply the common approach to develop a BACS in a safe and secure way and to operate it according to safety-security requirements. In addition, costs and effort are reduced compared to an independent safety and security development of a BACS. The reason is that the commonalities in the area of functional and non-functional measures are used. E.g., message overhead remains equal compared to a safety only message, but also security concerns are covered. Or, some test procedures and test tools are the same for safety and security. Finally, methods are given to handle conflicts and assess measures.

Customers benefit from the common approach because hopefully reduced development costs results in less expensive systems. Moreover, the structured and well described way of developing and maintaining increases the quality of the BACS in general. Furthermore, since the safety as well as the security standard define levels of the degree of safety (safety integrity level – SIL) and security (evaluation assurance level – EAL), respectively, customers get the chance of comparing various BAC systems regarding their safety and security features. Put another way, the common approach allows for a categorization of BAC systems.

Certification bodies such as TUV in Germany [TUD08] or Austria [TUA08] get the possibility to certify a system according to a well described set of requirements. Thus, customers are assured that requirements of a defined safety-security level are met. Room for interpretation and subjective perception at the certification bodies leading to different decisions as the case arises are reduced. Today there is no approach to the problem publically available. Certification in the area of BACS gains more and more importance, especially in Europe. It will become a legal requirement to use certified products in public projects [FIS04].

In conclusion, the common approach is new in the sense that is specifies the safety-security related harmonized activities for the whole system life based on well known standards. Integrated safety and security approaches are publically available on requirement level [EAM99] or on risk level [STO06], but not in detail for a complete lifecycle and not for building automation and control systems. Additionally, methods are specified by the author how to manage conflicts on requirement level and on function level. Two absolutely required tools in a common approach since conflicts are likely due to the different intentions of safety (risk reduction to people) and security (risk reduction to assets). The methods are verified and validated by examining concrete examples.

The common approach is applied to a defined use case in order to prove the concept: development and operation of a safe-secure BACS based on LonWorks. Although the use case is based on a specific BACS, most results are applicable for every BACS. It focuses on the safety-security requirements of a node including conflict resolution and measure assessment. A safe-secure requirement specification is specified. In addition, a safe-secure hardware and software design of a node is presented. Especially, the software design is discussed in more detail and safety-security functionality is outlined. In the end, the integration of a safe-secure node into the system is presented, in particular how to configure and commission a node by means of a remote network management device.

11.2 Further Procedure

The thesis presents a common approach to safety and security in BACS. It focuses on commonalities between safety and security in the primary lifecycle processes, and does not consider in detail supporting and organizational lifecycle processes. Future work will be to investigate the activities of the processes for commonalities. Related topics are for example how to organize and lay out the required documents. Additionally, conflict resolution and especially measure assessment may be adapted to these activities.

Another job going to be done is examining the other entities regarding safety and security, such as gateways and network management devices. How may the hardware and software architecture of a safe-secure gateway look like? What synergies can be gained by developing a safe-secure management tool? E.g., a password mechanism is integrated in a safety tool to avoid an accidental alteration of safety related data. It is stored in plaintext on the device. In contrast, security uses the password to get access to specific data and consequently the password must be stored secretly.

The common approach is being a great input to a working draft on functional safety and system security in BACS in European standardization. Since 2007 the working draft is treated as a working item in CEN [CEN08], Technical Committee (TC) 247, Working Group (WG) 4, called "Building Automation, Controls and Building Management" [CEN08]. The goal is to create an European and later on international standard for functional safety and system security in building automation and control systems. The standard ought to be application independent and a generic standard for safety and security in BACS.

For that reason a list of detailed requirements has to be set up for every process and every activitiy in the system life. Definitions for the different terms used must be found to establish a common understanding among the experts in the working group about the intention of the working draft. Generally, the idea of the common approach must be promoted in the BACS society. The first and most important argument against such an approach refers to the increasing costs, to the additional effort of training of integrators and operators. Related to the first argument it is said that customers will not buy such systems because of the costs and the complexity.

As a result, developers, manufactures, integrators and consumers have to be made aware of the safety-security needs. As a matter of fact, integration of different BAC systems and hence raising complexity, remote access to the systems, the use of new technology such as wireless networks, or the increasing demand of safety in our society simply result in new requirements on BACS. Of course, they were not considered when first automation systems were developed because at this time vertical integration, the Internet or Web services were beyond the scope.

Though, neglecting the new requirements does not help. Systems that are implemented in safety-security critical environments or that are providing safety-security critical services, and only these are the target systems of the common approach, should not be valued in terms of absolute costs. Other measures will be required to assess such systems. Maybe a way would be to assess the systems in terms of risk and costs resulting from a hazardous incident.

It is not just essential to ask for some understanding for a common approach. It is also required to specify a clear picture of the relationship between safety and security. When talking about safety together with security very often a relationship as shown in Fig. 11-2(a) is assumed. Security is considered to be supportive to safety on functional level. E.g., security measures are integrated in order to withstand also intentional attacks, and not only safeguard against stochastic and systematic failures. On the other hand, it is said that security can learn from safety on non-functional level. A typical example is presented in [BRO01]: a safety critical approach of designing a system is proposed for a security design. Or a safety method like the HAZOP analysis is modified to assess security in safety critical systems [WIN01].

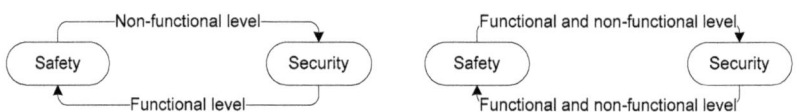

Fig. 11-2 (a) Obvious and (b) actual relationship between safety and security

However, safety and security have to be treated on equal basis. Not one is subordinated to another. Hence, safety can also learn from security on a non-functional level (Fig. 11-2 (b)). For example, in [RUS89] it is proposed to use the technique of security kernels, a small and simple component that encapsulates all security functionality, should also be used in the safety area. What is very little discussed is that safety actually supports security on functional level. An obvious example is redundancy. As mentioned in the thesis, a specific level of safety integrity can be reached by using redundant components, such as two microcontrollers (1oo2) or even three microcontrollers on a node (2oo3). The latter design increases data availability, a security objective, since corrupted data on one chip can be replaced by data from the other chip.

In short, the most important task in the near future is to convince the BACS society that such an approach is required in case of widening the field of application towards safety and security critical systems. Next, it is required to find a variety of examples that clearly show how such an approach works and to use them to finally receive a standard incorporating the common approach.

The thesis is not only the basis to finally receive a common approach in BAC systems. Its ideas and concepts are also applicable to IT systems in general. As mentioned in [PFI04], IT systems are integrated in more influential parts of our living- and working environment and these IT-systems are networked. They are safety and security critical and therefore also such systems should be developed and used based on the requirements of a common approach. The ideas presented in the thesis are the basis to reach the desired goals.

References on Scientific Publications

[ABD00]   M. Adballa, M. Bellare. Increasing the Lifetime of a Key: A Comparative Analysis of the Security of Re-keying Techniques. In *Proceedings of the 6th International Conference on the Theory and Application of Cryptology and Information Security: Advances in Cryptology*. Lecture Nodes in Computer Science, Vol. 1976, 2000.

[AMA07]   T. Tamandl, P. Preininger, T. Novak, P. Palensky. Testing approach for Online Self tests in Embedded Safety Related Systems. In *Proceedings of the 12th IEEE International Conference on Emerging Technologies and Factory Automation*, pp. 1270-1277, 2007.

[AME05]   S.H. Amer, J.W. Humphries, J.A. Hamilton Jr. Survey: Security in the System Development Lifecycle. In *Proceedings of the 2005 IEEE Workshop on Information Assurance and Security*, pp.310-316, 2005.

[AVI04]   A. Avižienis, J.C. Laprie, B. Randell, C. Landwehr. Basic Concepts and Taxonomy of Dependable and Secure Computing. In *IEEE Transactions on Dependable and Secure Computing*, Vol. 1, No. 1, pp.11-33, 2004.

[BAL98]   H. Balzert. *Lehrbuch der Software-Technik*. Heidelbert, Berlin, Spektrum Akademischer Verlag, 1998.

[BAT96]   W.F. Bates. Safety-related system design in power system control and management. In *Proceedings of the 4th International Conference on Power System Control and Management*, pp. 15-20, 1996.

[BAU00]   A. Bauer, A. Döderlein, P. Rössler. Fieldbus Systems for Home and Building Automation. *it+ti Infomrationstechnik und Technische Informatik*, Ausgabe 4, 2000.

[BOE04]   J. Börcsök. *Electronic Safety Systems*. Hüthig Verlag, Heidelberg, 2004.

[BOE07]   J. Börcsök. *Functional Safety – Basic Principles of Safety-Related Systems*. Hüthig Verlag, Heidelberg, 2007.

[BOE88]   B. W. Boehm, A spiral model of software development and enhancement. *IEEE Computer*, Vol. 21, No. 5, pp. 61-72, 1988.

[BRO01]   S. Brostoff, M. A. Sasse. Safe and Sound: A Safety-Critical Approach to Security. In *Proceedings of the 2001 Workshop on New Security Paradigms*, pp. 41-50, 2001.

[BRO93]   A.-P. Bröhl, W. Dröschel. *Das V-Modell: Der Standard für die Softwareentwicklung mit Praxisleitfaden*. München, Wien, Oldenburg, 1993.

[BUR92]   A. Burns, J. McDermid, J. Dobson. On the meaning of Safety and Security. *The Computer Journal*, Vol. 35, No. 1, pp. 3-15, 1992.

[DAL06]   International Electrotechnical Commission. *IEC 60929 – AC-supplied*

	electronic ballasts for tubular fluorescent lamps – Annex E: Control interface for controllable ballasts. IEC, 3rd Edition, 2006.
[DIE00]	D. Dietrich, W. Kastner, Th. Sauter (Publisher). *EIB Gebäudesbussystem*. Hüthig Verlag, Heidelberg, 2000.
[DIE97]	D. Dietrich, D. Loy, H. J. Schweinzer (Publisher). *LON-Technologie, Verteilte Systeme in der Anwendung*. Hüthig Verlag, Heidelberg, 1997.
[DZU05]	D. Dzung, M. Naedele, T. P. von Hoff, M. Crevatin. Security in Industrial Communication Systems. In *Proceedings of the IEEE*, Vol. 93, No.6, 2005.
[EAM99]	D.P. Eames, J. Moffett. The Integration of Safety and Security Requirements. In *SAFECOMP'99 Lecture Notes in Computer Sciences*, Vol. 1698, pp. 468-480, 1999.
[ECH02]	Echelon Corporation. *ShortStack User's Guide*. Version 2, 2002.
[EN149]	European Norm. *EN 14908 – Open data communication in building automation, controls and building management – control network protocol*. CEN, 2005.
[EN149-1]	European Norm. *EN 14908 – Open data communication in building automation, controls and building management – control network protocol – Part 1: Protocol Stack*. CEN, 2005.
[EN149-2]	European Norm. *EN 14908 – Open data communication in building automation, controls and building management – control network protocol – Part 2: Twisted Pair Communication*. CEN, 2005.
[EN500]	European Norm. *EN 50090 – Home and Building Electronic Systems (HBES)*. CENELEC, 1994.
[EN501]	European Norm. *EN 50126 – Railway applications. The specification and demonstration of reliability, maintainability and safety (RAMS)*. CENELEC, 1999.
[EN954-1]	European Norm. *EN 954 – Safety of Machinery, Safety related parts of control – Part 1: General Principles for design*. CEN, 1997.
[FIR03]	D. G. Firesmith. Common Concepts Underlying Safety, Security and Survivabily Engineering. *Technical Note CMU/SEI-2003-TN-033*, Carnegie Mellon University, 2003.
[FIS04]	P. Fischer, P. Palensky. The Importance of Being Certified – The role of conformance testing and certification of communication systems in building automation and control devices. In *Proceedings of the 7th IEEE AFRICON Conference in Africa*, pp. 1223-1228, 2004.
[FIS07]	P. Fischer, M. Holz, M. Mentzel. Network Management for a Safe Communication in an Unsafe Environment. In *Proceedings of the 5th IEEE International Conference on Industrial Informatics*, Vol. 1, pp. 131-136, 2007.
[FRU02]	K. Frühauf, J. Luedwig, H. Sandmayr. *Software-Projektmanagement und -Qualitätssicherung*. vdf Hochschulverlag AG, 4. Auflage, 2002.
[GER02]	Andreas Gerstinger, Gabriele Schedl, Werner Winkelbauer. Safety Versus Reliability: Different or Equal!? In *Proceedings of the 20th International System Safety Conference*, pp. 393-400, 2002.
[GIE95]	Gieck. *Technische Formelsammlung*. Gieck Verlag, 1995.

[GOR00] M. Gordeev. Security Architecture for Fieldbus Systems in the Internet Environment. *Ph.D. thesis*, Vienna University of Technology, Institute of Computer Technology, Austria, Vienna, 2000.

[GRA05] W. Granzer. Security in Networked Building Automation Systems. *M.S. thesis*, Vienna University of Technology, Institute of Computer Aided Automation, Automation System Group, Austria, Vienna, 2005.

[GRA06] W. Granzer, W. Kastner, G. Neugschwandtner, F. Praus. Security in networked building automation systems. In *Proceedings of the 2006 IEEE International Workshop on Factory Communication Systems*, pp. 283-292, 2006.

[HAM91] B.F. Hambling. Verification, Validation and the Achievement of Quality: A Holistic Approach. In *Proceedings of the 3rd International Conference on Software Engineering for Real Time Systems*, pp. 22-30, 1991.

[HER03] D. S. Herrmann. *Using the Common Criteria for IT Security Evaluation*. Auerbach Publications, 2003.

[HER08] J. Hertel. SafetyLon – an Innovative Concept to Bring the Features and Benefits of LON to the Safety Related Building Automation Market. *LonMark Magazine*, Vol. 4, Issue 1, 2008.

[HOE86] H. Hölscher, J. Rader, *Microcomputers in Safety Technique, An Aid to orientation for Developer and Manufacturer*. TÜV Rheinland, 1986.

[HOW87] W.E. Howden. *Functional Program Testing and Analysis*. McGraw-Hill, New York, 1987.

[IEC12] International Electrotechnical Commission. *IEC 12207 – Information technology – Software life cycle processes*. IEC, 1995.

[IEC13-1] International Electrotechnical Commission. *IEC 13335-1 – Information Technology – Guidelines for the Management of IT Security – Part 1: Concepts and Models for IT Security*. IEC, 1996.

[IEC15] International Electrotechnical Commission. *IEC 15408 – Information technology – Security technique – Evaluation criteria for IT security*. IEC, 2nd edition, 2005.

[IEC15-1] International Electrotechnical Commission. *IEC 15408 – Information technology – Security technique – Evaluation criteria for IT security – Part 1: Introduction and general model*. IEC, 2nd edition, 2005.

[IEC15-2] International Electrotechnical Commission. *IEC 15408 – Information technology – Security technique – Evaluation criteria for IT security – Part 2: Security functional requirements*. IEC, 2nd edition, 2005.

[IEC15-3] International Electrotechnical Commission. *IEC 15408 – Information technology – Security technique – Evaluation criteria for IT security – Part 3: Security assurance requirements*. IEC, 2nd edition, 2005.

[IEC54] International Electrotechnical Commission. *IEC 15446 – Information technology – Security techniques – Guide for the production of protection profiles and security targets*. IEC, 2001.

[IEC58] International Electrotechnical Commission. *Precision clock synchronization protocol for networks measurement and control systems*. IEC, 2004.

[IEC61] International Electrotechnical Commission. *IEC 61508 – Functional*

	safety of electric/electronic/programmable electronic safety-related systems. IEC, 1998.
[IEC61-0]	International Electrotechnical Commission. *Functional Safety and IEC 61508 – Part 0.* IEC, 2005.
[IEC61-1]	International Electrotechnical Commission. *IEC 61508 – Functional safety of electric/electronic/programmable electronic safety-related systems – Part 1: General Requirements.* IEC, 1998.
[IEC61-2]	International Electrotechnical Commission. *IEC 61508 – Functional safety of electric/electronic/programmable electronic safety-related systems – Part 2: Requirements for electrical/electronic/programmable electronic safety-related systems.* IEC, 2000.
[IEC61-3]	International Electrotechnical Commission. *IEC 61508 – Functional safety of electric/electronic/programmable electronic safety-related systems – Part 3: Software requirements.* IEC, 1998.
[IEC61-4]	International Electrotechnical Commission. *IEC 61508 – Functional safety of electric/electronic/programmable electronic safety-related systems – Part 4: Definitions and abbreviations.* IEC, 1998.
[IEC61-7]	International Electrotechnical Commission. *IEC 61508 – Functional safety of electric/electronic/programmable electronic safety-related systems – Part 7: Overview of techniques and measures.* IEC, 2000.
[IEC65]	International Electrotechnical Commission. *IEC 61511 – Functional safety – safety instrumented systems for the process industry sector.* IEC, 2003.
[IEC68]	International Electrotechnical Commission. *IEC 61158 – Digital data communication for measurement and control – Fieldbus for use in industrial control systems.* IEC, 2004.
[IEE10]	Institute of Electrical and Electronics Engineers Computer Society. *IEEE Standard for Software Verification and Validation.* IEEE Std 1012, 2004.
[IEE12]	Institute of Electrical and Electronics Engineers Computer Society. *IEEE Standard for Software Safety Plans.* IEEE Std 1228, 1994.
[IEE17]	Institute of Electrical and Electronics Engineers Computer Society. *IEEE Standard for Developing a Software Project Life Cycle Process.* IEEE Std. 1074, 2006.
[IEE74]	Institute of Electrical and Electronics Engineers Power Engineering Society. *IEEE Standard Criteria for Digital Computers in Safety Systems of Nuclear Power Generating Stations.* IEEE Std 7-4.3.2, 2003.
[IEE80]	Institute of Electrical and Electronics Engineers Computer Society. *IEEE Standard for Information technology – Telecommunications and information exchange between systems – Local and metropolitan area networks – Specific requirements; Part 15.4: Wireless Medium Access Control (MAC) and Physical Layer (PHY) – Specifications for Low-Rate Wireless Personal Area Networks (WPANs)*, IEEE Std. 802, 2006.
[IEE98]	Institute of Electrical and Electronics Engineers Computer Society. *IEEE Standard Dictionary of Measures of the Aspect of Dependability.* IEEE Std. 982.1, 2005.
[IEEC2]	Institute of Electrical and Electronics Engineers. *National Electrical Safety Code.* IEEE Std. C2, 2007.

[ISO16]   International Organization for Standardization. *ISO 16484-5 – Building automation and control systems (BACS) – Part 5: Data communication protocol.* ISO, 2003.

[ISO17]   International Organization for Standardization. *ISO 17799: Information technology – Code of practice for information security management.* ISO, 2000.

[ISO74]   International Organization for Standardization. *ISO 7498-1: Information technology – Open Systems Interconnection – Basic Reference Model: The Basic Model.* ISO, Part 1, 1994.

[ISO78]   International Organization for Standardization. *ISO 7816 – Identification cards – Integrated circuit(s) cards with contacts.* ISO, 1998.

[ITS91]   European Communities. *Information Technology Security Evaluation Criteria (ITSEC).* Version 1.2, 1991.

[KAS05]   W. Kastner, G. Neugschwandtner, S. Soucek, and H. M. Newman. Communication Systems for Building Automation and Control. In *Proceedings of the IEEE*, Vol. 93, no. 6, pp. 1178–1203, 2005.

[KER83]   A. Kerckhoff. La Cryptographie Militaire. *Journal des Sciences Militaires*, Vol. 9, pp. 5-38, and pp. 161-191, 1883.

[KNX04]   Konnex Association. *KNX Specifications.* Version 1.1., Belgium, 2004.

[KOO04]   Ph. Koopman, T. Chakravarty. Cyclic Redundancy Code (CRC) Polynomial Selection For Embedded Networks. In *Proceedings of the International Conference on Dependable Systems and Networks*, pp. 145-154, 2004.

[KOP97]   H. Kopetz. *Real-time Systems – Design Principles for Distributed Embedded Applications.* Kluwer Academic Publisher, 1997.

[KRA05]   H. R. Kranz. *BACnet Gebäudeautomation 1.4 – Die interoperable Gebäudeautomation.* Promotor Verlag, Karlsruhe, 2005.

[KRA94]   H. Krawczyk. LFSR-based Hashing and Authentication. In *Proceedings of the 14th Annual International Cryptology Conference on Advances in Cryptology*, LNCS Vol. 839, pp. 129-139, 1994.

[LAB95]   National Institute and Technology (NIST) (Computer Systems Laboratory). *Secure hash standard.* Federal Information Processing Standards Publication FIPS PUB 180-1, 1995.

[LAM98]   A. van Lamsweerde, R. Darimont, E. Letier. Managing Conflicts in Goal-Driven Requirements Enginnering. In *Transactions of the IEEE on Software Engineering*, Vol. 24, No. 11, 1998.

[LAP92]   J.C. Laprie (Editor). *Dependability: Basic Concepts and Terminology.* Springer Verlag, 1992.

[LAW00]   W. Lawrenz (Publisher). *CAN – Control Area Network – Grundlagen und Praxis.* Hüthig Verlag, Heidelberg, 4th edition, 2000.

[LEV95]   N.G. Leveson. *Safeware: System Safety and Computers.* Addison-Wesley, 1995.

[LIG02]   Liggesmeyer. *Software Qualität.* Spektrum Akademischer Verlag, 2002.

[LIP04]   St. Lipner. The Trustworthy Computing Security Development Lifecycle. In *Proceedings of the 20th Annual Computer Security Applications Confe-*

	rence, pp. 2-13, 2004.
[LOB05]	M. Lobashov. Applicability of Internet Protocols to Remote Fieldbus Access. *Ph.D. thesis*, Vienna University of Technology, Institute of Computer Technology, Austria, Vienna, 2005.
[LOY05]	LOYTEC. *LC3k Controller Family – User's Manual*, v1.2, 2005.
[MAH03]	St. Mahlknecht, P. Palensky. Linking Control Networks and Wireless Personal Area Networks. In *Proceedings of the 9th IEEE International Conference on Emerging Issues and Factory Automation*, Vol. 1, pp.31-36, 2003.
[MCG06]	G. McCraw. *Software Security – Building Security In*. Addison-Wesley, Boston, 2006.
[MOL02]	J.H. van Moll, J.C. Jacobs, B. Freimut, J.J.M. Trienekens. The Importance of Lifecycle Modeling to Defect Detection and Prevention. In *Proceedings of the 10th International Workshop on Software Technology and Engineering Practice*, pp. 144-155, 2002.
[MOT97]	Motorola. *LonWorks – Technology Device Data*. Revision 4, 1997
[NIS11]	National Institute of Standards and Technology (NIST). *Computer Data Authentication*. Federal Information Processing Standards FIPS 113, 1985.
[NIS19]	National Institute of Standards and Technology (NIST). *Advanced Encryption Standard*. Federal Information Processing Standards FIPS 197, 2001.
[NIS46-2]	National Institute of Standards and Technology (NIST). *Data Encryption Standard*. Federal Information Processing Standards FIPS 46-2, 1988.
[NIS46-3]	National Institute of Standards and Technology (NIST). *Data Encryption Standard*. Federal Information Processing Standards FIPS 46-2, 1999.
[NOV05]	T. Novak. Key Distribution in Power Line Networks. *M.S. thesis*, Vienna University of Technology, Institute of Computer Technology, Austria, Vienna, 2005.
[NOV07]	T. Novak, T. Tamandl. Architecture of a Safe Node for a Fieldbus system. In *Proceedings of the 5th IEEE International Conference on Industrial Informatics*, Vol. 1, pp. 101-106, 2007.
[ÖST07]	F. Österlind, E. Pramsten, D. Roberthson, J. Eriksson, N. Finne, T. Voigt. Integrating Building Automation Systems and Wireless Sensor Networks. In *Proceedings of the 12th IEEE International Conference on Emerging Technologies and Factory Automation*, pp. 1376-1379, 2007.
[OVA07]	T. Novak, A. Treytl, P. Palensky. Common Approach to Functional Safety and System Security in Building Automation and Control Systems. In *Proceedings of the 12th IEEE International Conference on Emerging Technologies and Factory Automation*, pp. 1141-1148, 2007.
[PAL00]	P. Palensky, Th. Sauter. Security Considerations for FAN-Internet Connections. In *Proceedings of the 2000 IEEE International Workshop on Factory Communication Systems*, pp. 27-35, 2000.
[PAL03]	P. Palensky. Smart Card Security for Field Area Networks. In *Proceedings of the IEEE Siberian Conference on Control and Communications*, pp. 135-138, 2003.
[PET07]	St. Petersen, P. Doyle, S. Vatland, Ch. S. Aasland, T. M. Andersen and

	D. Sjong. Requirements, Drivers and Analysis of Wireless Sensor Network Solutions for the Oil & Gas Industry. In *Proceedings of the 12th IEEE International Conference on Emerging Technologies and Factory Automation*, pp. 219-226, 2007.
[PFI04]	A. Pfitzmann. Why Safety and Security Should and Will Merge. In *SAFECOMP 2004 Lecture Notes in Computer Sciences*, Vol. 3219, pp. 1-2, 2004.
[PHO97]	Phoenix Contact (Publisher). *Grundkurs Sensor-Aktor-Feldbustechnik*. Vogel-Verlag, Würzburg, 1997.
[POO05]	E. R. Poort, P. H. N. de With. Resolving Requirement Conflicts through Non-Functional Decomposition. In *Proceedings of the 4th Working IEEE/IFIP Conference on Software Architecture*, pp. 145-154 , 2004.
[PRE06]	P. Preininger. Hardware Selftests For Safety Critical Fieldbus Nodes. *M.S. thesis*, Vienna University of Technology, Institute of Computer Technology, Austria, Vienna, 2006.
[RAN99]	W. Ranke, W. Effring. *Handbuch der Chipkarte*. Carl Hanser Verlag, 3. Auflage, München, Wien, 1999.
[REI98]	B. Reißenweber. Felbussysteme. R. Oldenburg Verlag, Münschen, Wien, 1998.
[REI01]	D. Reinert, M. Schaefer (Publisher). *Sichere Bussysteme in der Automation*. Hüthig Verlag, Heidelberg, 2001.
[REI07]	Ch. Reinisch, W. Kastner, G. Neugschwandtner, W. Granzer. Wireless Technologies in Home and Building Automation. In *Proceedings of the 5th IEEE International Conference on Industrial Informatics*, Vol. 1, pp. 93-98, 2007.
[REY05]	A. Treytl, T. Sauter, Ch. Schwaiger. Security Measures in Automation Systems – a Practice-oriented Approach. In *Proceedings of the 10th IEEE Conference on Emerging Technologies and Factory Automation*, Vol. 2, pp.847-855, 2005.
[ROY70]	W. Royce. Managing the development in large software systems. In *Proceedings of IEEE WESCOM*, 1970.
[RRP01]	UK Health and Safety Executive. *Reducing risk, protecting people (R2P2)*. HSE, 2001.
[RSA78]	R. Rivest, A. Shamir, L. Adleman. *A method for obtaining digital signatures and public-key cryptosystems*. Communication of the ACM, 21(2), 1978.
[RUS89]	J. Rushby. Kernels for Safety?. *Safe and Secure Computing Systems*, pp. 210-220, Blackwell Scientific Publications, 1989.
[SAU05]	Th. Sauter. Integration Aspects in Automation – a Technology Survey. In *Proceedings of the 10th IEEE Conference on Emerging Technologies and Factory Automation*, Vol. 2, pp.255-263, 2005.
[SCH00]	B. Schneier. *Secrets and Lies – Digital Security in a Networked World*. John Wiley & Sons, Inc., New York, 2000.
[SCH01]	Ch. Schwaiger, Th. Sauter. A Secure Architecture for Fieldbus/Internet Gateways. In *Proceedings of the 8th IEEE International Conference on*

[SCH02] *Emerging Technologies and Factory Automation*, Vol.1, pp.279-285, 2001.

[SCH02] Ch. Schwaiger, Th. Sauter. Security Strategies for Field Area Networks. In *Proceedings of 28th Annual Conference of the IEEE Industrial Electronics Society*, pp. 2915-2920, 2002.

[SCH03] Ch. Schwaiger, A. Treytl. Smart card based security for fieldbus systems. In *Proceeding of the 9th IEEE International Conference on Emerging Technologies and Factory Automation*, Vol. 1, pp. 398-406, 2003.

[SCH05] E. Schoitsch. Design for Safety and Security of Complex Embedded Systems: A Unified Approach. In *Cyberspace Security and Defense: Research Issues*, pp. 161-174, 2005.

[SCH96] B. Schneier. *Applied Cryptography*. John Wily & Sons, New York, 2nd edition, 1996.

[SEV07] B. Sevcik. Netzwerkzeitsynchronisation in sicheren Feldbussystemen. *M.S. thesis*, Vienna University of Technology, Institute of Computer Technology, Austria, Vienna, 2007.

[SMI04] D. J. Smith, K. G. L. Simpson. *Functional Safety – A straightforward guide to applying IEC 61508 and related standards*, Elsevier Butterworth-Heinemann, Oxford, 2nd edition, 2004.

[SOU07] S. Soucek, D. Loy. Vertical Integration in Building Automation Systems. In *Proceedings of the 5th IEEE International Conference on Industrial Informatics*, Vol. 1, pp. 81-86, 2007.

[STA03] W. Stallings. *Cryptography and Network Security*. Prentice Hall, 2003.

[STO02] G. Stoneburner, A. Goguen, A. Feringa. Risk Management Guide for Information Technology Systems. *Recommendations of the National Institute of Standards and Technology (NIST)*, NIST Special Publication 800-30, 2002.

[STO06] G. Stoneburner. Toward a unified security-safety model. *IEEE Computer*, Vol. 39, pp. 96-97, 2006.

[TAM07] T. Tamandl, P. Preininger. Online Self Tests for Microcontrollers in Safety Related Systems. In *Proceedings of the 5th IEEE International Conference on Industrial Informatics*, Vol. 1, pp. 137-142, 2007.

[TAN03] A. S. Tanenbaum. *Computer Networks*. Prentice Hall, 4th edition, 2003.

[TCS85] US Department of Defense. *Trusted Computer System Evaluation Criteria (TCSEC)*. DoD 5200.28-STD, National Computer Security Center, 1985.

[TOR92] UK Health and Safety Executive. *Tolerability of risk for nuclear power stations (TOR)*. HSE, 1992.

[TRE04] A. Treytl, Th. Sauter, Ch. Schwaiger. Security Measures for Industrial Fieldbus Systems – State of the Art and Solutions for IP-based Approaches. In *Proceedings of the 2004 IEEE International Workshop on Factory Communication Systems*, pp. 201-209, 2004.

[TRE05] A. Treytl, T. Novak. Practical Issues on Key Distribution in Power Line Networks. In *Proceedings of the 10th IEEE International Conference on Emerging Technologies and Factory Automation*, Vol. 2, pp. 83-90, 2005.

[WAN05] L. Wang, K. Ch. Tan. Software Testing for Safety-Critical Applications.

[WIN01] *IEEE Instrumentation & Measurement Magazine*, pp. 38-45, June 2005.
R. Winther, O-A. Johnsen, B. A. Gran. Security Assessments of Safety Critical Systems Using HAZOPs. In *SAFECOMP 2001 Lecture Notes in Computer Sciences*, Vol. 2187, pp. 14-24, 2001.

[WIT95] A. Witter. Entwicklung eines Modells zur optimierten Nutzung des Wissenspotenzials einer Prozess-FMEA. In *Forschungsberichte VDI*, Reihe 20, Nr. 176, 1995.

[WOL01] W. Wolf. *Computers as Components, Principles of Embedded Computing System Design*. Morgan Kaufman Publishers, 2001.

[WOO07] C. Woody, Ch. Alberts. Considering Operational Security Risk during System Development. *IEEE Security and Privacy*, IEEE Computer Society, No. 01, 2007.

[WRA05] P. Wratil. Sichere Netzwerke – Technik und Anwendung, Teil 1: Fehlerarten und Korrekturstrategien. *Elektronik*, Vol. 21, 2005.

[WRA07] P. Wratil, M. Kieviet. *Sicherheitstechnik für Komponenten und Systeme*. Hüthig Verlag, Heidelberg, 2007.

[ZAF05] S. Zafar, R. G. Dromey. Integrating Safety and Security Requirements into Design of an Embedded System. In *Proceedings of the 12th Asia-Pacific Software Engineering Conference*, 8 pp., 2005.

[ZEL98] H. Zeltwanger. *Can-das serielle Bussystem – vom Auto in die Industrie*. PRAXIS Profiline, Vogel Verlag, 1998.

[ZUS01] W. Zuser, St. Biffl, T. Grechenig, M. Köhle. *Software Engineering mit UML und dem Unified Process*. Pearson Studium, Munich, Germany, 2001.

Internet References

[CEN08]	European Committee for Standardization. Available at http://www.cen.eu/cenorm/homepage.htm [18/05/2008].
[RFC22]	The Internet Society. *Request for Comments (RFC) 2246 – The TLS Protocol*. Version 1.0, 1999. Available at http://rfc.net/rfc2246.html [27/03/2008].
[RFC43]	The Internet Society. *Request for Comments (RFC) 4330 – Simple Network Time Protocol (SNTP)*. Version 4, 2006. Available at http://rfc.net/rfc4330.html [21/03/2008].
[RFC47]	The IETF Trust. *Request for Comments (RFC) 4772 – Security Implications of Using the Data Encryption Standard (DES)*. December 2006. Available at http://rfc.net/rfc4772.html [21/04/2008].
[RFC49]	The IETF Trust. *Request for Comments (RFC) 4949 – Internet Security Glossary*. Version 2, 2007. Available at http://rfc.net/rfc4949.html [21/03/2008].
[TUD08]	Technischer Überwachungsverein Deutschland. Available at http://www.tuev.de [06/06/2008].
[TUA08]	Technischer Überwachungsverein Österreich. Available at http://www.tuev.at [06/06/2008].

Die VDM Verlagsservicegesellschaft sucht für wissenschaftliche Verlage abgeschlossene und herausragende

Dissertationen, Habilitationen, Diplomarbeiten, Master Theses, Magisterarbeiten usw.

für die kostenlose Publikation als Fachbuch.

Sie verfügen über eine Arbeit, die hohen inhaltlichen und formalen Ansprüchen genügt, und haben Interesse an einer honorarvergüteten Publikation?

Dann senden Sie bitte erste Informationen über sich und Ihre Arbeit per Email an *info@vdm-vsg.de*.

Sie erhalten kurzfristig unser Feedback!

VDM Verlagsservicegesellschaft mbH
Dudweiler Landstr. 99
D - 66123 Saarbrücken
www.vdm-vsg.de

Telefon +49 681 3720 174
Fax   +49 681 3720 1749

Die VDM Verlagsservicegesellschaft mbH vertritt

Printed by Books on Demand GmbH, Norderstedt / Germany